FATHER
DIVINE

FATHER DIVINE

❧

Robert Weisbrot

Senior Consulting Editor
Nathan Irvin Huggins
Director
W.E.B. Du Bois Institute for Afro-American Research
Harvard University

CHELSEA HOUSE PUBLISHERS
New York   Philadelphia

Chelsea House Publishers
Editor-in-Chief   Remmel Nunn
Managing Editor   Karyn Gullen Browne
Copy Chief   Mark Rifkin
Picture Editor   Adrian G. Allen
Art Director   Maria Epes
Assistant Art Director   Noreen Romano
Manufacturing Director   Gerald Levine
Systems Manager   Lindsey Ottman
Production Manager   Joseph Romano
Production Coordinator   Marie Claire Cebrián

Black Americans of Achievement
Senior Editor   Richard Rennert

Staff for FATHER DIVINE
Text Editor   Marian W. Taylor
Copy Editor   Christopher Duffy
Editorial Assistant   Michele Haddad
Designers   Ghila Krajzman and Diana Blume
Picture Researcher   Patricia Burns
Cover Illustration   Bill Donahey

First Printing

1 3 5 7 9 8 6 4 2

Library of Congress Cataloging-in-Publication Data
Weisbrot, Robert.
   Father Divine, religious leader/by Robert Weisbrot
   p.   cm.—(Black Americans of achievement)
   Includes bibliographical references and index.
Summary: Examines the life and career of the black religious leader
who founded the Peace Mission Movement, which worked to end
poverty, racial discrimination, and war and which did much to provide
for the poor during the Depression.
ISBN 0-7910-1122-4
      0-7910-1147-X (pbk.)
1. Father Divine—Juvenile literature. 2. Peace Mission
Movement—Juvenile literature. 3. Afro-American clergy—
Biography—Juvenile literature. 4. Father Divine. [1. Clergy.
2. Afro-Americans—Biography.] I. Title. II. Series.
BX7350.Z8F378 1991   91-3639
[B]   CIP
299'.93—dc20   AC

Frontispiece: *Father Divine,
midcentury America's most
celebrated black evangelist, works
with staff members at his New York
City headquarters in the late 1930s.*

CONTENTS

BLACK AMERICANS OF ACHIEVEMENT

RALPH ABERNATHY
civil rights leader

MUHAMMAD ALI
heavyweight champion

RICHARD ALLEN
religious leader and social activist

LOUIS ARMSTRONG
musician

ARTHUR ASHE
tennis great

JOSEPHINE BAKER
entertainer

JAMES BALDWIN
author

BENJAMIN BANNEKER
scientist and mathematician

AMIRI BARAKA
poet and playwright

COUNT BASIE
bandleader and composer

ROMARE BEARDEN
artist

JAMES BECKWOURTH
frontiersman

MARY MCLEOD BETHUNE
educator

BLANCHE BRUCE
politician

RALPH BUNCHE
diplomat

GEORGE WASHINGTON CARVER
botanist

CHARLES CHESNUTT
author

BILL COSBY
entertainer

PAUL CUFFE
merchant and abolitionist

FATHER DIVINE
religious leader

FREDERICK DOUGLASS
abolitionist editor

CHARLES DREW
physician

W.E.B. DU BOIS
scholar and activist

PAUL LAURENCE DUNBAR
poet

KATHERINE DUNHAM
dancer and choreographer

DUKE ELLINGTON
bandleader and composer

RALPH ELLISON
author

JULIUS ERVING
basketball great

JAMES FARMER
civil rights leader

ELLA FITZGERALD
singer

MARCUS GARVEY
black nationalist leader

DIZZY GILLESPIE
musician

PRINCE HALL
social reformer

W. C. HANDY
father of the blues

WILLIAM HASTIE
educator and politician

MATTHEW HENSON
explorer

CHESTER HIMES
author

BILLIE HOLIDAY
singer

JOHN HOPE
educator

LENA HORNE
entertainer

LANGSTON HUGHES
poet

ZORA NEALE HURSTON
author

JESSE JACKSON
civil rights leader and politician

JACK JOHNSON
heavyweight champion

JAMES WELDON JOHNSON
author

SCOTT JOPLIN
composer

BARBARA JORDAN
politician

MARTIN LUTHER KING, JR.
civil rights leader

ALAIN LOCKE
scholar and educator

JOE LOUIS
heavyweight champion

RONALD MCNAIR
astronaut

MALCOLM X
militant black leader

THURGOOD MARSHALL
Supreme Court justice

ELIJAH MUHAMMAD
religious leader

JESSE OWENS
champion athlete

CHARLIE PARKER
musician

GORDON PARKS
photographer

SIDNEY POITIER
actor

ADAM CLAYTON POWELL, JR.
political leader

COLIN POWELL
military leader

LEONTYNE PRICE
opera singer

A. PHILIP RANDOLPH
labor leader

PAUL ROBESON
singer and actor

JACKIE ROBINSON
baseball great

BILL RUSSELL
basketball great

JOHN RUSSWURM
publisher

SOJOURNER TRUTH
antislavery activist

HARRIET TUBMAN
antislavery activist

NAT TURNER
slave revolt leader

DENMARK VESEY
slave revolt leader

ALICE WALKER
author

MADAM C. J. WALKER
entrepreneur

BOOKER T. WASHINGTON
educator

WALTER WHITE
civil rights leader

RICHARD WRIGHT
author

ON
ACHIEVEMENT

—————— ❦ ——————

Coretta Scott King

BEFORE YOU BEGIN this book, I hope you will ask yourself what the word *excellence* means to you. I think that it's a question we should all ask, and keep asking as we grow older and change. Because the truest answer to it should never change. When you think of excellence, perhaps you think of success at work; or of becoming wealthy; or meeting the right person, getting married, and having a good family life.

Those important goals are worth striving for, but there is a better way to look at excellence. As Martin Luther King, Jr., said in one of his last sermons, "I want you to be first in love. I want you to be first in moral excellence. I want you to be first in generosity. If you want to be important, wonderful. If you want to be great, wonderful. But recognize that he who is greatest among you shall be your servant."

My husband, Martin Luther King, Jr., knew that the true meaning of achievement is service. When I met him, in 1952, he was already ordained as a Baptist preacher and was working toward a doctoral degree at Boston University. I was studying at the New England Conservatory and dreamed of accomplishments in music. We married a year later, and after I graduated the following year we moved to Montgomery, Alabama. We didn't know it then, but our notions of achievement were about to undergo a dramatic change.

You may have read or heard about what happened next. What began with the boycott of a local bus line grew into a national movement, and by the time he was assassinated in 1968 my husband had fashioned a black movement powerful enough to shatter forever the practice of racial segregation. What you may not have read about is where he got his method for resisting injustice without compromising his religious beliefs.

He adopted the strategy of nonviolence from a man of a different race, who lived in a different country, and even practiced a different religion. The man was Mahatma Gandhi, the great leader of India, who devoted his life to serving humanity in the spirit of love and nonviolence. It was in these principles that Martin discovered his method for social reform. More than anything else, those two principles were the key to his achievements.

This book is about black Americans who served society through the excellence of their achievements. It forms a part of the rich history of black men and women in America—a history of stunning accomplishments in every field of human endeavor, from literature and art to science, industry, education, diplomacy, athletics, juris-prudence, even polar exploration.

Not all of the people in this history had the same ideals, but I think you will find something that all of them had in common. Like Martin Luther King, Jr., they all decided to become "drum majors" and serve humanity. In that principle—whether it was expressed in books, in-ventions, or song—they found something outside themselves to use as a goal and a guide. Something that showed them a way to serve others, instead of only living for themselves.

Reading the stories of these courageous men and women not only helps us discover the principles that we will use to guide our own lives but also teaches us about our black heritage and about America itself. It is crucial for us to know the heroes and heroines of our history and to realize that the price we paid in our struggle for equality in America was dear. But we must also understand that we have gotten as far as we have partly because America's democratic system and ideals made it possible.

We are still struggling with racism and prejudice. But the great men and women in this series are a tribute to the spirit of our democratic ideals and the system in which they have flourished. And that makes their stories special and worth knowing. ❧

FATHER
DIVINE

1

THE TRIAL

THE REVEREND MAJOR J. Divine, more popularly known as Father Divine, was arrested in late 1931 while leading an interracial religious service in Sayville, a small town 40 miles east of New York City. A short, balding man in his early fifties, he was no ordinary prisoner.

In the span of just a few years, Father Divine had achieved legendary status among hundreds of poor ghetto dwellers. He provided magnificent Sunday banquets during the worst depression in American history: An endless succession of fine foods was served free of charge all day and evening at the minister's spacious home in Sayville, with awestruck visitors entering, eating, singing hymns, and leaving as they pleased. Sometimes a guest might offer a donation, in which case Divine would return it with the mysterious assurance "God will provide."

Nor was this the only mystery to Father Divine's far-reaching leadership. In an age when racial segregation was the rule in nearly all social aspects of American life, particularly in such personal matters

Father Divine is flanked by his first wife, Mother Divine, as he returns the enthusiastic greetings of supporters in the late 1930s. Also known as the Reverend Major J. Divine, he preached that all people contained the spirit of God and should live in harmony and equality.

as dining and worship, the crowds at Divine's religious feasts featured an increasing number of white faces. The minister thought this interracial mingling highly desirable; as he explained it, all people contained the spirit of God, and therefore they should live in harmony and equality. In 1931, that was a dangerous philosophy to preach—and still more dangerous to practice.

Father Divine was the only black homeowner in Sayville, and despite episodes of racism, he had generally been tolerated as polite and hardworking. But his hospitality to largely black crowds during the Great Depression brought complaints by white neighbors that he was making Sayville a "Negro haven" and a "Harlem colony." The Suffolk County district attorney commissioned an undercover investigation of Divine's finances and morals in the hope of finding some basis for ridding Sayville of his presence. Two attractive women from Harlem pretended to join the following and, in the most flamboyant tradition of espionage, used every means from eavesdropping to attempted seduction to find the secret of his wealth. All in vain, the female investigators reported. Divine had fed them, sheltered them, treated them kindly in all ways, and asked nothing in return.

Further investigations also failed to find evidence of any wrongdoing. Yet Sayville's white residents still wanted Father Divine out of their town.

Late one Sunday night in November 1931, neighbors complained to the authorities that the religious singing at Divine's home had become a nuisance. Five deputy sheriffs, half a dozen state troopers, and firemen carrying hoses were sent to break up the worship. The minister promised to surrender his entire congregation to the police. Then he and 80 followers left voluntarily for the town hall to answer for their excessively loud praying.

It is likely that Divine would have worked out a compromise with his neighbors had noise been the sole source of conflict. But racial matters were at issue. Even though Sayville's white residents said they had no complaint about the moral character of Father Divine and his followers, they wanted him to relocate to another town.

Father Divine, for one, was certain that racism was at the root of his ordeal. He said later that from the time he moved into Sayville, certain prejudiced people had sought any pretext to oppose his residence in the community. "They said my car disturbed them when I would start it up," he recalled. "They said many different things were disturbances, and I said to them, 'Yes, my success and my prosperity disturb you.'"

The minister was not alone in tracing Sayville's actions to racial prejudice. James C. Thomas, a distinguished black attorney, volunteered his services

In Philadelphia to make a speech, Divine joins his wife in an open car (center) as reporters and believers strain for a closer view. Divine set a formidable standard of social activism that other ministers, well aware of his popularity, tried to match.

on behalf of Father Divine because "to allow an incident of this nature to go unchallenged is to weaken the foundations of democracy in the United States and to single out the Negro group as one not entitled to full enjoyment of every right . . . guaranteed by the Constitution."

Harlem, which boasted New York City's largest black community, had provided a growing number of

"I am returning to my fold with new vigor and a firmer grip upon the teachings of the Almighty," Divine said upon learning that his 1932 conviction for disturbing the peace was being overturned. The reason for his arrest was that he had incensed white bigots by leading an interracial religious service in Sayville, New York.

Sunday pilgrims to Divine's Sayville home; these people now began to rally on the minister's behalf. Crowds of up to 10,000 pressed to hear Divine preach at rallies to protest against his arrest and impending trial. An observer reported that not since the appearance of Marcus Garvey, a popular black nationalist leader during the 1920s, had Harlem witnessed "so spontaneous a mass demonstration and such religious fervor as has greeted the appearance of Father Divine." He was by now far more than a religious leader; he had become a symbol of black hopes and resentment against racial injustice.

The case of *Sayville v. Divine* came to court in May 1932. A glance at the charges confirms that racial prejudice lay behind much of the hostility toward Divine and his followers. Although the general charge was "maintaining a public nuisance," the bill of particulars included among its accusations that the defendant "conducted so-called religious services, at which services colored and white people did congregate and mingle together in large numbers." In this way, indeed, Father Divine was willfully disturbing the peace.

The presiding judge, Lewis J. Smith, was a stern figure of great honesty, considerably less tolerance, and no apparent humor. He had earned a reputation for handing down maximum sentences, and in his private life his avoidance of emotional display in religion was a world apart from the rollicking prayer sessions and cultlike worship of Divine's following. Smith took an instant dislike to Father Divine. He actively assisted the prosecution and questioned witnesses harshly about the racial mixing in Divine's congregation.

Attorney Thomas continually objected to Smith's high-handed manner, but the judge predictably overruled him each time. To Smith, the defendant was in some way evil and dangerous, and this justified suspension of the most elementary legal safeguards.

The jury quickly agreed that Father Divine was guilty of being a public nuisance. It also recommended leniency, but Judge Smith would not hear of it. After letting Divine languish in jail for two weeks before sentencing, he declared that he had "information that this man is not a moral man but immoral. I believe that he is not a useful member of society but a menace to society." Smith then added for good measure that Divine had even deceived his own lawyer into believing him. It was a mock trial to the end.

Having found Divine, in effect, guilty of "menace," Smith disregarded the pleas for leniency and gave the maximum sentence of one year in jail and a $500 fine. The defendant accepted this with a quiet dignity that impressed many in the courtroom. Yet it was a time that tested his faith in God's will and his own mission, and the tensions showed. A reporter watched the authorities lead Divine off to jail as his disciples called out to him, "Peace, brother!" Divine, said one observer, "looked at them with a mingled expression of confidence and wounded despair, and passed on."

Few of Divine's supporters were so restrained. Some, who had earlier warned Judge Smith against having Father Divine spend even a single day in jail, now loudly predicted that Smith, for daring to oppose the power of God Almighty, would die. A black journal, the *Amsterdam News*, asserted more rationally but with equal resentment: "The principal charge against him seems to have been his color, and Mr. Justice Smith is not deceiving us about it. . . . Prosecution and persecution are different."

At this juncture, Judge Smith displayed an uncharacteristic flair for the dramatic. In an act perhaps more influential than any in his long and

active career, he changed the course of cult history when, three days after sentencing Divine, he suddenly keeled over, dead. He was 56 years old and had been in apparent excellent health during the evening preceding his death. One suspects that the trial had taken its toll on his physical and emotional wellbeing; to many who had watched Father Divine's career in awe, there seemed more direct causes for Smith's abrupt end.

Father Divine betrayed no doubts or surprise when informed of Smith's sudden demise. Previously, despite his assurances of his willingness to stay in jail, Divine had seemed to visitors somewhat nervous and apprehensive. Now, however, he was again in full command. Controlling whatever emotion he may have experienced upon hearing of Smith's death, Divine reportedly paused a moment and then said sadly, "I hated to do it."

Divine (rear, center) presides over one of the free feasts that earned him both fame and followers during the Great Depression of the 1930s. At the time, the presence of whites and blacks at the same table shocked many Americans.

On June 24, the minister was released from prison on bail, and his exit was as flamboyant as his entry and brief stay. A reporter described him as "nattily dressed in a blue serge suit, blue shirt and blue tie, and his hair was trimmed and his face freshly shaved. He thanked the warden for the many courtesies extended him . . . and told the sheriff that, even in the face of persecution and execution, he was prepared to 'do the same thing over again.'" Inmates of the prison sang and shouted as Divine waved his farewell. "You are taking away a good man," one of them told Thomas.

Soon after his release from jail, Father Divine relocated in Harlem, the heart of his following. He explained his departure from Sayville in generous terms, observing that he would not stay where he was unwelcome. Yet even if residents had reconsidered their attitudes toward him, he would probably have found some other reason for his change of address, for Sayville could no longer provide a setting large enough for the deeds of its newly famous pastor.

As word spread of Divine's miraculous powers, clusters of converts formed in widely scattered locales and dedicated themselves to the Father's cause. Their centers became known collectively as the Peace Mission, a possible reference to Divine's teachings on inner bliss and the value of interracial harmony. This informal christening signaled that the minister now led a significant social movement; its ideals were still developing, but its numbers and enthusiasm were fast making its leader a figure of national renown.

On January 9, 1933, Divine's triumph became complete when a New York appeals court agreed unanimously that his trial had been marred by gross prejudice and overturned the verdict. The trial was also crucial to Divine's career because of its effect on the inner man. Unlike some of history's religious mystics who, in desperate circumstances, wondered if

Providence had not, after all, forsaken them, the minister had held fast to his sense of mission both in the courtroom and in prison. Now, having wrestled with this supreme test of faith, he felt an overwhelming sense of conviction about his role as a special instrument of the Lord.

Fittingly, Divine's first act upon release on bail was to greet James Thomas with cries of "Peace!" and declare to him, "I am returning to my fold with new vigor and a firmer grip upon the teachings of the Almighty." Father Divine's messianic ministry had begun in earnest. ❧

2

THE RISE OF FATHER DIVINE

FATHER DIVINE ALWAYS refused to discuss the early years of his life, when he went by the name of George Baker, perhaps because he found it too common for someone who had gone on to achieve such a powerful identity. In any event, the scholar Jill Marie Watts, sifting through old census reports, recently discovered that Baker was born in 1879 in Rockville, Maryland, 14 years after slavery had been abolished in the United States. This and other accounts of his origins agree that Baker grew up somewhere in the South, when cities and states throughout the region were passing laws to segregate and humble blacks in all areas of life.

In Maryland, as in the rest of the South, Jim Crow laws excluded blacks from white schools, train cars, hotels, theaters, bathrooms, and other public facilities. These laws also kept most blacks from voting, required them to tip their hat when they met whites on the street, and directed blacks who entered white homes to do so only through the back door. Because dining was considered an intimate social activity among equals, blacks were forbidden to dine

George Baker, the man who would become Father Divine, was born in Rockville, Maryland (pictured in the early 20th century), in 1879.

in the same restaurant as whites. Countless insults of this sort led Baker, when he was an adult, to proclaim a mission to "break down the wall" separating the races so that all people could at last live together in dignity.

In the absence of opportunities to improve his life through a good education or a high-paying job, Baker—like many southern blacks—poured his energy into religion. His curious and open nature felt wonderment at the pomp and passion of the black church service. He traveled often, assisting preachers in all parts of the country, and took in the atmosphere of piety, the enthusiasm of the worshipers, and, above all, the preacher's art. Baker saw that black preachers had a challenging task: addressing an audience of little education. Generally having only slightly more learning themselves, the preachers looked for creative ways to get their message across. Sometimes they would create their own words to convey ideas about God's mysterious nature and powers. In their sermons, they would often act out the roles of various biblical figures, from Moses to Jesus Christ, as a way to make the stories of the Bible meaningful to modern audiences. No one in the Scriptures, including God, was so distant as to be beyond the ability of a first-rate preacher to act out.

Some educated middle-class worshipers, black as well as white, might laugh at such practices or even find them offensive. But a sermon that conveyed a biblical message with such personal intensity could have a powerful effect on its listeners.

Baker knew that an effective preacher did much more than inform; he brought forth from his congregants shouts and gestures of pious enthusiasm. A southern black church service typically ended in outcries of emotion. Worshipers—mostly women— flung themselves into the aisles, some shrieking, others "possessed" by the spirit, and all bursting with

Southern churchgoers respond to a rousing sermon with tinkling tambourines, rhythmic hand-clapping, and shouts of "Amen!" The South's black churches, with their highly charged emotions and intense spiritual involvement, served as a training ground for the future Father Divine.

"Hallelujahs" and "Amens" that showed their faith in Jesus.

By the time he became known as Father Divine, Baker had absorbed many new religious experiences. Yet he always retained the basic style and technique of these inventive southern black preachers. He learned their emotional approach to religion, their creation of new words in sermons, their role-playing and ability to preach as if personally speaking for God, and their stirring of an audience to "feel" the Lord's salvation.

Most important, Baker felt a sense of the liberating power that the church held for even the most downtrodden of God's children. Most black churches avoided trouble with the wider society over racial matters, and Baker himself could not yet see clearly how to bring religion into a struggle against injustice. Still, he burned inwardly with visions of God tearing down all barriers between people, black and white.

As a young man at the turn of the century, Baker worked as a hedge cutter in Baltimore, Maryland, and taught Sunday school in a black Baptist church. Like others at the church's prayer meetings on Wednesday evenings, he sometimes rose to give informal sermons. He spoke about God being present everywhere, a large idea that he explored with large words of his own making: "God is not only personified and materialized. He is repersonified and rematerialized. He rematerializes and He rematerialates." These speeches, however unconventional their use of language, conveyed Baker's central belief that the pious must seek God in all things, not simply in a remote "Heaven."

Baker even then could draw a crowd. Such a commanding presence could not be explained by his appearance alone: His broad shoulders and chest rested on a small frame, and he seemed to most observers scarcely five feet tall. Yet he possessed a powerful voice, a sure command of the Bible, and a flair for improvising sermons. Add to this a gaze through almond-shaped eyes that could be at once kindly and hypnotic, and one can picture a man who—even at this early stage of his vocation—was able to capture audiences by sharing his sense of God's presence in the world.

In 1906, Baker met two self-proclaimed men of God who had a lasting impact on his understanding of religion and his own purpose in life. One was John Hickerson, who preferred the title Reverend St. John Divine Bishop and who had earlier joined many religious cult movements. The other was a luckless preacher named Samuel Morris. He had a special talent for provoking congregations to expel him physically from their church services by attempting to tell them of his divinity at the most ill-timed moments.

Morris was filled with an extra measure of the religious piety common in the rural South. He had moved to Allegheny City, Pennsylvania, at the time he discovered a key passage in the Bible (from St. Paul's first letter to the people of Corinth), "Know ye not that ye are the temple of God, and that the spirit of God dwelleth in you?" Morris read, amazed by the verse, which seemed to him to be saying that he himself was God. He subsequently set out for the black churches of Baltimore, where he was determined to tell the congregants his momentous news.

In one church after another, Morris went to the podium and, without warning, spread his arms wide and shouted, "I am the Father Eternal!" The congregants were not favorably impressed. Each time Morris proudly announced himself as God Almighty, he would find himself getting tossed into the street, never to return to that particular church.

On one occasion, Morris was helped to his feet by a lone believer, 27-year-old George Baker, who invited the preacher to his home in a boardinghouse. Baker became a disciple of Morris's, helped him obtain a job driving a wagon, and began to hold several weekly prayer meetings for 10 to 20 people.

Morris soon took to referring to himself as Father Jehovia; Baker, in keeping with his role as a prophet for Morris, adopted his own title, the Messenger. For all their claims of divine status, the two caused little stir in Baltimore. Both men carried to extremes an established tradition among rural blacks—the intense identification with words of Scripture. They remained within a carefully limited circle of sympathizers, continued to earn money in conventional ways, and, in all other respects, led lawful and conservative lives. They therefore escaped the unfriendly attention of the authorities and the residents at large.

What did Baker see in the work of Morris, whose boasts of being God had previously won only contempt from whole congregations? The young Baker was seeking support for his belief in human worth regardless of race or origin. Here now was Morris, announcing to all listeners, no matter how seemingly humble, "The spirit of God dwelleth in you." For Baker, ardently pious and still highly impressionable, this idea may have deepened both his

Marcus Moziah Garvey (1887–1940), the Jamaican-born black nationalist leader, founded the Universal Negro Improvement Association (UNIA) in 1914. Like Divine, Garvey believed that the achievement of black economic independence would lead to the attainment of black civil rights.

belief in God's presence and his sense of religion as a force for equality.

The influence of John Hickerson led Baker to start preaching on his own as the Messenger. Hickerson was a veteran of religious movements such as the Pentecostal Holiness; Holy Rolling; Elder Robinson's Live Ever, Die Never Church in Boston; and others. He too became a disciple of Morris's but eventually objected to his leader's claim that he alone held the highest level of godliness. Morris may have assumed that the verse in St. Paul's letter had special relevance to him as its "discoverer," but as Hickerson reasoned, every person contained equally the light of God within his or her soul.

After Hickerson's protest, the trio's days together were numbered. In 1912, Baker and Hickerson left Morris, each to preach on his own. Hickerson established the modestly successful Church of the Living God in New York City, while Baker headed south, without disclosing his exact plans to anyone.

Preaching under such names as the Messenger and the Son of Righteousness, Baker drew crowds with his promise that a better life was coming—not simply in an afterlife but on this earth—and that all people shared equally in the spirit of God. Many listeners viewed him as a godlike prophet, a reaction that naturally alarmed both established black pastors and local authorities.

In 1914, two black ministers in Valdosta, Georgia, who were jealous of Baker's influence accused him of blasphemy (the act of claiming the attributes of God). In response, white authorities, alarmed that a black man who preached of a better life on earth was being treated as divine by other blacks, had Baker arrested. The writ against him listed his identity as "John Doe, alias God." Baker had clearly been taking Samuel Morris's doctrines to heart.

While in the Valdosta jail, the Messenger received a call from J. R. Moseley, a white writer on

Thousands of admiring Harlemites applaud a 1920 UNIA parade. Although Divine shared many of Marcus Garvey's hopes and ideas, he shunned the high-profile political approach of the UNIA, preferring to deal directly with individuals and their spiritual and material needs.

philosophy and religion. Moseley was visiting a professor in Valdosta when his curiosity had been excited by rumors of a man claiming to be God. More intent to question than to condemn, Moseley found himself engaged in an animated discussion with the "bright-faced" prisoner. Moseley asked Baker if he was not denying his own name and history and identity so that he might become entirely receptive to God's presence. The prisoner replied, "You understand me better than anyone else." Moseley offered to act as Baker's attorney and to give him financial aid. The prisoner explained that he did not accept money but that he would be glad to have bread "to share with his fellow inmates."

The Messenger's new attorney developed a deep respect for his client. "There was about the man an unmistakable quiet power that manifested itself to anyone who came in contact with him," Moseley later recalled. "He told me that he tried to do God's will" and that "he thought that to the extent that he could identify himself with God, he was God."

Baker was tried for blasphemy, found "of unsound mind" but innocent of any offense, and freed on condition that he leave Georgia immediately. Among the personal belongings returned to the reprieved man were 2 news clippings, one stating that he had served 60 days on a chain gang in Savannah and another about the wreck of a car filled with prison inspectors. In the margin of this second article someone had written, "Be sure your sins will find you out." This sentiment coincides with the preachings of Father Divine 20 years later, which spoke of retribution at work in every car crash and other misfortune.

The newly freed evangelist soon ran into further intolerance. His preaching offended some residents in another Georgia town, and he was placed in a state mental institution. It may have been this otherwise unexplained incident, rather than the trial in Valdosta, that Father Divine referred to during the 1930s: "Many years ago, I was called in question among great ministers and bishops, etc., who desired to hold me for insanity."

Baker persuaded the warden there to write to J. R. Moseley, who vouched for the preacher's good character and emotional health. The Messenger was released a few days later, upon complying with the asylum's regulation that he first adopt a "human" name. He chose John, although it is not clear whether he did so in reference to some long-discarded identity, a biblical character, or simply a slyly ironic abbreviation of his legal identity in Valdosta: "John Doe, alias God."

Prodded by memories of arrest and imprisonment, Baker left Georgia and began a leisurely journey north. Along the way, he gathered a few loyal disciples as he preached on street corners and occasionally in black churches. Around 1915, he arrived in New York City, then fast becoming the center of black American culture and religious life.

The spiritual and social world that Baker entered was rapidly changing. An influx of southern black farmers into the northern cities was adding greatly to the population of all the major ghettos. This brought a spectacular rise in the number of urban black churches, as the migrants relied heavily on religion to help ease the adjustment to a new environment. New York City, for example, had only 13 black churches in 1865, a number that increased slowly until the main period of migration, when it sky-rocketed to approximately 200 by the 1920s.

For poor, uneducated migrants who did not feel comfortable with the established churches and more high-toned congregations, countless informal groups welcomed them to services in vacant storefronts, where their prayers preserved the passionate quality of the rural black southern churches they had left behind. The newcomers were often drawn to various black cults, whose worship centered on a leader of extraordinary personal magnetism. The cult leader typically presented himself as a special ambassador of God and, as such, inspired intense displays of pious emotion. The cult leader's unquestioned authority also provided a sense of order and guidance for many uprooted people who could not easily cope with the cold, impersonal atmosphere of city life.

In 1915, the Messenger was a little-known cult figure. He led a handful of disciples and avoided

Unemployed men share a soup-kitchen meal during one of America's periodic economic depressions. In the years of the Great Depression—by far the nation's worst—Divine fed thousands of hungry people at his headquarters in Sayville, New York.

involvement in major social issues. Civil rights groups, such as the recently formed National Association for the Advancement of Colored People (NAACP), failed to attract his notice. Not even the appearance later in the decade of the fiery West Indian–born Marcus Garvey, who spoke of a dawn of black liberation and the rise of Africa, drew Baker's interest. He was a man clearly intent on a rest from the controversy and occasional persecution that marked his past.

By 1919, the Messenger was ready for yet another change—or, rather, series of changes. First, he purchased a new, spacious home in the all-white community of Sayville on Long Island. (Such opportunities for blacks to enter white neighborhoods were rare; this one came about when a townsman decided to spite a neighbor he disliked by selling his home to a black buyer.)

A second change in Baker's life was to formalize a partnership with a female disciple named Pinninah, whose name joined his on the deed of sale. Whereas the evangelist had long advocated a chaste life, he found in Pinninah a valuable assistant and loyal admirer who affirmed his own sense of special destiny. Somewhat older than the Messenger and at least a head taller, she nevertheless seemed to play a relatively passive role in their relationship.

Finally, the *Messenger* disappeared in favor of a new symbolic identity, Major J. Divine, the *Major* possibly reflecting the popularity of military titles in the aftermath of World War I. His few disciples lived communally, sharing all income from jobs that Divine obtained for them by vouching for their honesty and diligence as cooks, domestic workers, and so forth. As his prosperity grew, he began to host free banquets and religious services on Sundays, but the number of worshipers at his home grew rather slowly through the 1920s.

Divine delivers an impassioned sermon during one of his Sayville feasts. Many of the era's cult leaders decked themselves in theatrical splendor, but Divine always wore the neat, unadventurous attire of a conventional businessman.

The journeys Divine had taken to this point suggest a man still seeking his special role. As George Baker, he had earned a respectable place in lower-middle-class black society. As the Messenger, he had brought the tidings of God's presence in every man, until jail and the threat of further repression led him to take a more conservative course. Now, in Sayville, he prepared to assume two identities at once. To the outside world, he was known only as a quiet, upright member of the community; to his inner circle of disciples, he was the embodiment of God on earth. His symbolic rebirth as Major J. Divine, combining the patriotic and the heavenly, reflected his new and quite successful dual life.

The onset of the Great Depression in late 1929 ended this period of quiet withdrawal from the outside world. By 1930, the economic catastrophe had thrown millions of Americans into poverty and unemployment. More than 50 breadlines and a dozen private agencies for the homeless operated in New York City alone, yet they could relieve only a small part of the growing hardship. In nearby Sayville, the continued prosperity and hospitality of the Reverend Major J. Divine began to take on a larger-than-life quality. The number of guests at his Sunday feasts multiplied, and visitors began to whisper about Father's mysterious powers.

As startling as Father Divine's generosity was the thoroughly unexotic manner with which he presided over these gatherings. Divine displayed no religious relics or altars in his home, furnishing it instead in the manner of a typical suburban homeowner. And he had no use for the flowing robes, turbans, and other colorful clothing worn by so many faith healers, mystics, and other cult leaders. Father Divine instead preferred a plain business suit and tie, which did not suggest a mysterious prophet so much as a down-to-earth, conservative philanthropist.

The "Divine touch" did not lack technique. Although he assured all who inquired about his source of funds that "God will provide," the minister took practical steps not to waste God's bounty. Rather than serve all the food at once, he had waitresses first bring out pitchers of water, tea, and other beverages while he poured coffee for the guests. All were encouraged to drink freely while talking and singing hymns. Only after much time had elapsed did the first solid food appear, mainly starches and perhaps some fruits and vegetables. By the time the meats arrived, visitors had already eaten much of the less expensive food. The roasts passed back and forth impressively across the table, then were often reclaimed fairly intact, to be frozen for future use.

As Divine gained experience dealing with the crowds, the showman in him also blossomed. The playwright Owen Dodson recalled that he and his older brother visited Divine's Sayville home and were struck by an apparent miracle—an endless supply of milk that poured from the spigot of a large dispenser on the table. Young Owen was much impressed, but at meal's end his curious brother peeked under the extremely long tablecloth and discovered two youths pumping energetically at an apparatus hidden beneath the table. Of course, many would have considered it miracle enough to provide milk without limit or charge in a time of widespread hardship. But the minister, having already warmed to his image as divine father, was not taking any chances.

Father Divine might have remained relatively unknown had he been among many other pastors who greatly aided the poor and unemployed. During the Depression, poor blacks everywhere depended on their churches—the most important institution in the black community—to provide economic relief. Yet during the early years of the Depression most ministers still displayed a largely otherworldly outlook, and their efforts for the poor and unemployed were limited. Divine's ministry to the needy therefore helped fill an important gap in church activity; it also rapidly made him one of the ghetto's most prominent religious figures.

As his fame grew, Father Divine became more outspoken about how true religion should center on ending poverty and racism rather than on what a faraway Heaven might be like. Indeed, he insisted, the failures of the old, otherworldly religion made his presence necessary: "Because your god would not feed the people, I came and I am feeding them. Because your god kept such as you segregated and discriminated [against], I came and I am unifying all nations together. That is why I came, because I did not believe in your god."

By word and deed, Father Divine was calling the black church back to earth. As he expressed his driving religious mission to his followers in Harlem, "I shall not be discouraged until I emancipate all humanity."

3

THE PEACE MISSION

❦

EVEN BEFORE THE sensational trial of Father Divine in 1932 gained national headlines, his Peace Mission movement had begun to attract a far-flung network of disciples. Word of mouth about Divine's ministry was amplified by Harlem newspapers, whose editors knew that stories on this colorful and controversial leader boosted sales. Outside the ghettos, Divine's sermons and sayings reached new converts through journals published by followers in Los Angeles. A British philosopher named Walter Lanyon further extended Divine's appeal with several volumes that rendered the minister's colloquial speech into formal English. These books reached educated religious seekers, some of whom founded Peace Mission centers overseas.

The Peace Mission welcomed Americans of every social background, economic level, and racial group. When critics charged that the movement led people to depend too much on Father Divine, he insisted that he was, instead, healing the weak. Calling himself a social and spiritual doctor and his

A trio of Peace Mission members attend a Philadelphia mass meeting in the early 1930s. Divine's awed disciples often credited him with turning their life around: "All my life I didn't amount to nothing," said one woman, "but since I come to know Father is God, I'm important."

Divine, three of his five secretaries, and a male aide, Brother Lamb, tackle a pile of correspondence in their Harlem office. Most Peace Mission members were black and female, but Divine—a strong advocate of racial and sexual equality—also attracted a large number of whites and males.

movement a "hospital," he said: "Those who come to me are sick and afflicted. . . . They are seeking some information; they are seeking some help and some aid; they are seeking some deliverance from certain conditions, if it is only mentally . . . they are seeking something." Indeed, for all their differences, those who followed Father Divine were nearly all, on some level, people in crisis.

Lower-class black ghetto dwellers formed a majority of the Peace Mission members during the Depression. In New York and New Jersey, states that contained the heart of Father Divine's support, the following was 85 to 90 percent black. Even in states farther west, blacks were almost never less than a third of the disciples in any Peace Mission center.

Father Divine attracted black ghetto residents in part because he was an inspiring role model for many poor, uneducated blacks seeking evidence that they could improve their lives. Divine was one of them—a dark-skinned evangelical preacher with an earthy humor, informal speech, and a southern accent. Yet he was also a man of amazing powers, planning deals involving millions of dollars, giving to charity with funds from unknown sources, and challenging white authority with a boldness and success that was surely miraculous.

In joining the Peace Mission, members often found a new sense of self-respect. A woman reborn as Beautiful Faith spoke for many followers in saying, "Father Divine gave me my first chance to be somebody. All my life I didn't amount to nothing— just cooking and cleaning for the white folks. But since I come to know Father is God, I'm important. I'm a dietitian in God's kitchen."

Other followers found the proof of Divine's greatness in his help when hard times and racial prejudice had left them without work. June Peace, a secretary in the Peace Mission, recalled that during the Depression the refusal of whites to employ her had made her bitter, but Father Divine quickly provided her with a job and "loved all the bitterness away." A powerfully built disciple serving as a chauffeur for Father Divine told how he was once unable to get work in his native Newark: "But Father Divine gave me a job, he solved my problem. He can solve all your problems."

Women formed between three-quarters and nine-tenths of the Peace Mission's national membership, an overwhelming proportion that was also true of many other cult movements attracting blacks. Unlike the wider society, in which women were treated with lower status than men, the Peace Mission valued equally the devotion of men and women. Women were treated as equals with men in prayer, at the banquet table, and in running the Peace Mission's various branches. Divine's secretaries—positions of responsibility—were mostly women. So too were the majority of cashiers and supervisors, who handled large sums of money in the Peace Mission branches.

The chief aide and most honored disciple of Father Divine during the 1930s was a black woman named Faithful Mary. Born Viola Wilson, she had lived in Newark as a sickly vagabond until meeting Father Divine in 1934. Then she suddenly blossomed into a glowing, vigorous woman of nearly 200 pounds, beaming good health to all she met. To the many ghetto residents who knew of her once gaunt appearance, Faithful Mary became a special symbol of Father Divine's saving power. Because she spoke passionately about Father Divine's effect on her life, she was given the rare privilege of preaching on Divine's behalf to distant Peace Mission branches.

Many of the female converts were divorced, widowed, abandoned, or in some other way at a particularly lonely and vulnerable point. Typically, they welcomed Divine's principle of celibacy as a path to renewal by channeling their devotion to a higher cause, a welcoming community, and a loving Father.

On occasion, the new converts abandoned their families to join the Peace Mission, and this led to several widely publicized trials at which husbands angrily blamed Father Divine for inducing their wives to desert them. Divine explained in court that in fact he counseled husbands and wives to remain together, but chastely, and that the movement cared for all children of disciples. These emotionally wrenching cases did not seriously affect the Peace Mission's operations, but they revealed the extent to which some followers had severed old social ties in embracing the movement.

Other groups that were economically or socially insecure also contributed sizable shares to the Peace

Mission membership. A majority of members, for example, were elderly people, at a time when economic hardship was most severe for the aged. (The practice of giving Social Security pensions for the elderly did not begin until 1935, and the fear of poverty in old age could be terrifying.) West Indian immigrants, who often were discriminated against by native black Americans, sometimes found in cult movements the acceptance they could not obtain in American society.

Recent southern migrants to the northern cities also flocked to the Peace Mission. Scorned by long-settled ghetto residents as ignorant and ill mannered, they found a sense of security as followers of Father Divine. That Divine himself was obviously of southern origin and enjoyed telling stories referring to life in the South added to their feelings of belonging.

Faithful Mary, dubbed "Father Divine's prize miracle" by the press, addresses a Peace Mission meeting in 1936. At this point sleek and radiant, Mary had weighed only 97 pounds and suffered from tuberculosis when she met Divine 2 years earlier.

These branches of Divine's Universal Peace Mission were among an estimated 150 such outposts across the United States. In its heyday, the Mission also boasted some two dozen extensions in Canada, western Europe, and Australia.

Not all the disciples of Father Divine were poor, ill, or victims of racism. Some were simply seeking a religious experience that gave them lasting comfort. Other converts were drawn by Father Divine's ideas about equality. In an era when young men especially felt encouraged to reform society, the Peace Mission's communal life and its stand for racial justice drew more than a few idealists. A number of white reformers in California, for example, published a newspaper, called the *Spoken Word*, about the Peace Mission's activities. This journal looked forward to the day when "millions of Peace restaurants" and other interracial, communal shops would give all people a fair share of the nation's wealth.

Whether people came to Father Divine for food, jobs, spiritual truth, social leadership, healing, or shelter from any of dozens of personal troubles, they soon left behind their old identities. They adopted a strict code of discipline, often took a new "spiritual name" to symbolize their religious rebirth, and learned to live for "the cause" and for Father Divine.

How large was the kingdom Father Divine ruled? Because there were no official membership records and because one did not have to be a regular member to visit a Peace Mission center, share Divine's hospitality, and hear him preach, no one could say with certainty just how many followers he had. Some reports claimed that Divine had millions of disciples, and Divine himself estimated that 22 million people followed his ministry. This figure, however, almost surely inflated the total by more than 99 percent. Based on attendance at banquets and on such indirect evidence as the number of registered voters with "spiritual" names, it is likely that there were fewer than 10,000 hard-core supporters, although such a reputable journal as *Time* reported in 1937 that 50,000 followers might be closer to the mark.

What is certain is that word of Father Divine's leadership spread throughout the United States and to several foreign nations during the 1930s. The number of Peace Mission branches multiplied in the early years of the decade to a peak of around 150 to 160, a figure sustained through the early 1940s. In 1936, when the Peace Mission was at the height of its popularity and influence, an official directory showed that more than a quarter of all branches were located in New York State, indicating the importance of Harlem and neighboring black districts as a source of recruitment. Among businesses that advertised in the major Peace Mission newspaper, a large majority were based in New York City.

The only area of the country with few Peace Mission branches was the South. The Peace Mission listed only 12 centers in the former Confederate states in 1940, or about 7 percent of the total. The reasons include the obvious danger of believing in racial integration and equality, plus the fact that Father Divine did not often visit the South, either because of bitter past experiences or his busy life in Harlem.

It is unclear whether any of the southern centers except those in Florida were interracial, which might well have led authorities to close them down. If any Peace Mission members in the South ever demonstrated on behalf of social reform, let alone integration, no record of such an act of courage exists. Father Divine, in effect, conceded that any popular movement for racial equality in his native region would have to wait for the struggles of a later generation.

More than two dozen Peace Mission centers operated outside the United States during the 1930s, mainly in Canada, western Europe, and Australia. Most were led by English-speaking men or women who had visited Father Divine or read his sermons and felt called to preach in their native countries. The scope of Divine's influence, indeed, ranged far. Disciples at his headquarters at 20 West 115th Street in Harlem liked to show visitors a postcard on display at their center. It was sent from China and addressed: "God—Harlem—U.S.A." These few words were sufficient identification for postal workers to deliver the card without delay to Father Divine.

In forming new Peace Mission branches, disciples applied Father Divine's principles of communal living, racial integration, and chaste conduct between men and women. The larger Peace Mission centers served as dormitories for the members, with blacks and whites mingling freely but men and women

Participants in a 1936 New York City parade proudly escort a chair decorated with a picture of their absent leader. Divine's followers always reserved him a place—an apartment in a branch center, a seat at the table, the place of honor in a procession—whether they expected his actual presence or not.

assigned to separate halls. These buildings also provided assembly rooms, kitchens, and dining rooms. A special "studio" was almost always set apart for Father Divine, no matter how unlikely the chance that he would ever avail himself of this architectural tithe. Most centers were in the poorer sections of a city and were scarcely luxury buildings. But the rooms were kept "scrupulously clean," a visitor observed, and complied with the city's health regulations.

The most devoted of Father Divine's disciples were known as Angels. They donated their wages or labor to the movement and in return received food, shelter, and clothing. Father Divine's Children, who formed perhaps three-quarters of the membership, were not quite as committed to the movement: They observed Father Divine's teachings and paid to live in the Peace Mission residences but kept their private property.

In a movement that strongly emphasized social equality, there were no sharp differences in the treatment of Angels and Children. Anyone who wanted could become an Angel simply by living communally without reservation; that is, by sharing everything. No special uniforms, medals, certificates, or rank distinguished any members, nor were Father Divine's aides given a great deal of authority over other disciples.

Far more than American society, the Peace Mission provided equal opportunities for blacks and whites. On the one hand, many of the most educated and skilled members were white, including all Father Divine's secretaries during the 1930s and most of the lawyers. Whites also contributed greatly to the Peace Mission newspapers. On the other hand, Faithful Mary, a poor black woman with a police record, became Divine's second-in-command for several years. Mother Divine, the minister's wife—and highly honored in the movement—was also black. So was

Divine's attorney, Arthur Madison, who may well have been his single most trusted counselor.

The egalitarian spirit of the movement was perfectly captured by Ross Humble, a prominent follower who gave up a lucrative practice as a psychologist in California to serve the Peace Mission free of charge. When asked in 1935 about his race, he objected to being classified as white, repeated his devotion to the principles of Father Divine, and reminded the interviewer, a reporter for a Harlem newspaper, that none of Divine's followers was ever distinguished by "complexion."

The Peace Mission's greatest safeguard against rigid divisions among the membership was perhaps that Father Divine was viewed by all as the one leader of surpassing wisdom and authority. Followers acknowledged Father as a divine savior, shaped their lives around his wishes, and based their self-esteem on his kindness and encouragement. Outsiders might doubt his claims to divinity, but there is little question that within the realm of the Peace Mission, Father Divine truly reigned supreme.

The vast Peace Mission network rested to a remarkable degree on Father Divine's energy and his organizing flair. Typically, he would rise just after dawn and review transcripts of his speeches for publication. Then, after a "snack" of six scrambled eggs, pancakes, sausage, fried potatoes, and coffee, Divine would whirl through activities from morning into the late night: negotiating purchases, dictating letters, meeting reporters and visitors seeking counsel, supervising the administration of his various centers, singing hymns and dining with his flock, and preaching on matters ranging from spiritual consciousness to the bills currently before Congress.

What drove him? Some critics, pointing to the Peace Mission movement's multimillion-dollar businesses and landholdings, scoffed that Divine—like

many other cult leaders—cared less for being a prophet than making a profit. Newspapers commonly portrayed him as a luxury-loving racketeer who sported dozens of silk suits, had a fleet of chauffeur-driven limousines, and enjoyed hovering above his parading followers in a private plane.

Divine certainly had access to great wealth through the contributions of disciples, some of whom were extremely affluent. Yet on closer inspection, the image of Divine as a selfish, reckless spender appears largely a myth, though one nourished in part by the minister's own flamboyant manner.

Like other cult leaders of the Depression era, Father Divine knew that displays of luxury conveyed an aura of success and power, and he often flashed the trappings of great personal wealth. Yet the limousines, often described in newspapers as costing $40,000, were actually dilapidated models acquired for a few hundred dollars by disciples who donated or loaned them for Divine's use. The silk suits were purchased for $7.50 each at a bargain store and altered for Divine's short frame by followers who were seamstresses. Even his famed monoplane was rented

Parked outside a Philadelphia Peace Mission office, Divine's car draws the attention of a curious passerby. Reporters often commented on the evangelist's extravagant vehicles, but most were old and all were donated by disciples.

Staff members join Divine (second from left) on a flying trip. The press insisted on calling the aircraft "the Harlem messiah's private plane," but in truth it was owned by a rental company and leased for Divine's occasional use.

for special occasions at modest rates. Despite appearing to be a man who always went first-class, Divine in practice valued the wisdom of acquiring goods secondhand.

The evidence suggests, too, that Divine did not simply hoard his wealth but instead distributed it amply among his disciples. One can measure this, first, in legal terms: All the Peace Mission's extensive property was deeded to his followers, not to Divine personally. (This, too, had its controversial side: Father Divine avoided payment of income taxes by stating that he personally owned no property, a claim that investigators for the Internal Revenue Service furiously but vainly tried to disprove.) More important in practical terms was the evident rise in living standards enjoyed by the mass of Divine's disciples, many of whom found in the Peace Mission their first taste of security against hunger and homelessness during the Depression.

The desire for power is another motive often cited to explain Father Divine's behavior. "Father Divine is God," his followers declared, to the minister's evident approval. This notion drew smiles or sneers from the educated and angry sermons from clergymen throughout Harlem. Of course, his theology was more complex—every person might display the divine spirit—and Divine himself assured disciples, "Each of you can become as I am." Still, even the most sophisticated of Divine's disciples believed that Father alone had achieved perfect unity with the divine spirit.

Divine's large ego seemed wholly comfortable with the grateful worship of his followers, many of whom found in him a source of strength and hope. In 1934, several learned disciples asked him, "How can you teach that you are God?" Divine was unruffled. He explained that if by believing he was God people were led to reform their lives and raise themselves up, "Who am I to discourage them?"

Divine's aura of divinity was in any case scarcely unique: Poor ghetto neighborhoods during the Depression produced scores of religious figures who rose to prominence by claiming to represent God on earth and promising an escape from misery and insecurity. What set Divine's ministry apart was the degree to which he pursued goals larger than personal power or wealth. Unwilling simply to bask in the adulation and donations of his followers, he directed their enthusiasm outward, in favor of the reform causes he valued: racial integration, equal rights, and economic cooperation to end poverty. In glorifying Father Divine, therefore, the Peace Mission cult also glorified his crusade for a new social order. ❧

4

FEASTING AT THE
PEACE MISSION

❦

FATHER DIVINE EXERTED a strong, though
sharply mixed, impact on black Americans during the
Depression. As the cult head of a largely poor and
ill-educated following, he embarrassed the more
refined elements of ghetto society. Ministers of
conventional churches especially feared his Peace
Mission movement as a bad influence on their
congregants. At the same time, however, Divine
impressed all but the most blindly critical with his
social achievements, which imparted a luster to his
ministry few orthodox pastors could match. As a
result, he symbolized for many black leaders the
possibilities of a movement for civil rights reform
through the churches, even though some of these
same people viewed him as at best a marginally
respectable figure.

Pastors of conventional churches were by far the
group most hostile toward Father Divine. They
resented his appeal to many of their congregants, and
they saw his brand of religion as an affront to their
own. These sentiments, which had surfaced while
Divine was still a fledgling leader in Sayville, grew

*Mother Divine passes her husband a plate of fried chicken during a
1937 banquet. The evangelist refused all offers of payment for his
celebrated public meals: "God will provide," he assured his guests.*

harsher as the Peace Mission extended across Harlem and other ghettos.

The Reverend E. W. White, who in 1933 told his fellow Baptist ministers that Father Divine should be jailed for "99 years and a few more days," set the tone of most clerical speeches on Divine throughout the Depression decade. Ministers at that conference joined in condemning Divine and all religious figures who "conceal themselves behind the cloak of the ministry" to engage in "racketeering."

Clergymen particularly despised what they saw as a mockery of traditional worship by Father Divine and other cult figures. One minister said that when he went by a Peace Mission center, he heard the Angels singing parodies of well-known hymns and parading with placards, all declaring that "Father Divine Is God." To this minister and many others, Divine instead appeared as the Devil, tempting people away from their own churches and from true Christian faith.

Much of the disdain for Father Divine further stemmed from the fact that his critics were mainly educated and middle class and his followers were mostly poor, uneducated, and unpolished. The force of such class differences is apparent from the cold reception Father Divine's followers received in 1934, upon purchasing a home in the exclusive Harlem neighborhood known as Striver's Row. Possibly the newcomers expected that the affluent black professionals of Striver's Row would welcome them as similarly hardworking, law abiding, and devoted to winning full civil rights for all citizens. But almost from the outset, when a sign in blazing red and blue letters proclaimed "Peace" to all the cultured inhabitants of Striver's Row, the Peace Mission members outraged the neighborhood with their uncontained enthusiasm and evident lower-class background.

Divine kicks off a banquet with his dinner bell. Skeptics sneered at the evangelist as a "fraud" or even a "devil." But his disciples' beaming faces, recorded in picture after picture, suggest that he was providing what his flock needed and wanted: spiritual comfort, physical well-being, and a sense of dignity and self-worth.

Even from the fringe of established black society, Father Divine's ministry substantially aided the development of new religious patterns in the ghettos. His ability to attract congregants from the conventional churches helped awaken pastors to the need for practical social programs to benefit the masses. So, too, did the fact that lay leaders frequently praised his ministry as a model of civil rights activism to which other clergymen should aspire. Thus, while Divine largely failed to gain the clergy's personal approval, he still helped prod them to greater social activism: For only by expanding their commitment to racial equality and care for the poor could these ministers maintain their stature in the black community.

Even when targeted for criticism by other ministers, Father Divine remained a formidable challenge simply by continuing to help the needy. The Reverend L. K. Williams, who presided at the major black Baptist convention of 1939, devoted his keynote speech to denouncing Father Divine, warning his fellow ministers, "You cannot build a religion on a bread-and-butter brigade." Williams received hearty applause, but to his keen embarrassment, he could not prevent scores of attending Baptist pastors from flocking to the nearby Peace Mission center throughout the week in order to take advantage of the inexpensive food and lodgings. For 15 cents these preachers, many of them living on very modest earnings, enjoyed meals at the Peace Mission as nourishing as the one the convention sold for 50 cents. The episode led Harlem's leading journal to ask whether the old, purely spiritual outlook of the black churches any longer sufficed in the changing ghetto communities.

The banquet table was the center of communal activity in every Peace Mission branch. There hundreds gathered to praise Father Divine's generosity while enjoying feasts of extraordinary splendor. The seating of whites and blacks together at the table—a rare experience even in the North—vividly illustrated Divine's insistence on racial equality and harmony among his followers. The sharing of the meals themselves had, of course, a special meaning in these Depression years, affirming that those of faith would prosper even when times seemed hard. The banquets also represented a timeless aspect of

Unperturbed by other clergymen's stinging criticism of his "bread-and-butter" approach to religion, Divine (seated, center rear) hosts yet another huge feast for the needy. Diners often expressed their delight by rhythmically clapping their hands and shouting, "Ain't that wonderful?"

religious life: the search for God through human fellowship and devotion to a common spiritual leader.

The praise sessions at these banquets, as one visitor observed, were scenes of "emotional release, frenzied handclapping, yelling back and forth, dancing, hustle and bustle of young and old." Fervent singing went on for hours, recalling the old slave spirituals.

The scholar Guy Johnson observed that these songs, like the spirituals, were "accompanied by handclapping, footpatting, swaying, and sometimes by a sort of shuffling dance." Some tunes resembled African "shout songs," and lyrics often sprang from sudden religious enthusiasm. A man telling how Father Divine lifted his burdens "became very emotional and spoke in a sort of rhythmic sing-song fashion. He finally started something which became a song. Swinging his body and patting his feet, he said, 'He is making us like our Savior in this world.' After he had repeated this several times other people began to take up the refrain line . . . and shortly they were singing rather heartily to a tune which was very similar to 'She'll Be Coming 'Round the Mountain When She Comes.' The followers themselves insisted that the songs were created on the spot and that the reason they were not printed was that, in the words of a woman follower, 'They are outpourings of the spirit.'"

The banquets were a time not only for songs and shouts of praise but also for the most personal confessions of past sins and pledges to sin no more. Many told of renouncing a life of crime, liquor, or adultery. Speakers commonly referred to Father Divine as one would talk of a conscience. A woman given to mystic visions claimed that Father "certainly worked on me. . . . He is the only god who has kept me from playing cards, from being an adulteress." Another described him as the one influence that could restrain her from evil: "I used to do every wrong thing. I was first class at everything. I had two husbands and nobody could clean me up. Father Divine came and saved me. Father Divine is God."

A big, powerfully built man on the platform spoke in a husky voice about the many former criminals he spotted in the banquet hall: "You've never seen an audience like this at any convention or conference unless they had to have policemen. [Now] freely you come and freely you are seated. Now, ain't that wonderful?"

The speaker told of having been a drunkard and gambler before Father Divine had inspired him to give up his vices. "Here we have God with us, walking and talking just like us. Isn't that wonderful?" he exclaimed. Shouts of joy met his remarks, which explained much of the mystery surrounding Father Divine's hold over these people. For all were indeed searching for a god and guide they could feel befriended by and could even, when Father Divine attended a banquet, personally address.

The banquets of course provided abundant physical as well as spiritual nourishment. A typical banquet featured 50 courses and on some occasions as many as 200. Each guest at the banquets served him- or herself as large a portion of every item as he or she wanted, then passed the dish on to a neighbor. All knew that the very poor need never pay for this food, which was paid for through the donations of wealthier members. In the midst of the Depression, such generosity helped many members survive and became a symbol of Father Divine's preaching about building a Heaven on earth.

Of the many descriptions of these seemingly limitless feasts, the most captivating is given by Charles Braden, a student of religion who visited frequently with Father Divine. His account is from 1945 but is similar in all respects to the many records of earlier feasts:

Eleven different cooked vegetables passed in quick succession: steamed rice, green beans, green peas, boiled succotash, stewed tomatoes, lima beans, greens, and carrots. I, not knowing what to expect, had begun by taking a little bit of everything but soon saw that this was not wise and became more selective. Then came platters of meat. It will be recalled that this experience was still in wartime [World War II] and rationing had not yet been lifted. First came three or four cold cuts, including baked ham. Then appeared the hot, freshly cooked meats: roast beef, beef curry, meat loaf, fried chicken, roast duck, roast turkey, beef steak, each heaped high on the platters which were passed around the festive board. Then came salads: fruit salad containing Persian melon, cantaloupe, alligator pears, and lettuce, and sliced tomato salad. Next came bread: hot corn bread, hot rolls, white bread, brown bread, rye bread, raisin bread, and for good measure, crackers, accompanied by a good serving of butter. There was cranberry sauce for the roast turkey, apple sauce for the duck, and jams and jellies in profusion. The drinks consisted of iced tea, iced coffee, and iced water. I was assured that I could have hot coffee if I wanted it. Dessert consisted of two kinds of cake, one of them with fruit and whipped cream. On another like occasion, great heaping bowls of ice cream of two or three flavors were circulated around the table. Along with all of this went sweet pickles, mixed pickles, ripe olives, green olives, and all the condiments that would ordinarily be served on such an occasion. The average number of different dishes served at these banquets is around fifty-five.

Divine strikes a serious note during an after-dinner sermon. Whatever his subject—hilarious stories about the South, racial prejudice, or "Heaven on earth"—the minister maintained an almost uncanny control of his audience, creating any mood he chose.

The tale of Jesus feeding the multitudes scarcely seemed more miraculous to Peace Mission members than their own awesome feasts, huge enough to convince thousands in the nation's poorest slums that Father Divine was truly God on earth.

When Divine himself appeared at a banquet, sometimes after hours of anticipation, the noise level became deafening. The cheering continued for minutes after he had made his way to the far end of a U-shaped table in the center of the hall. All the while the Father's expressive eyes looked out with kindness, approval, and a certain wistfulness at these people who came to him for meaning.

To many who had been slipping in the most basic struggle for survival, this would take the form of meals and shelter in his care, when no government or private relief agencies reached them. To others, spiritual searchers or those escaping from personal tragedy, the Father's kindly gaze and words were the meaning their lives required. To all, this was a Peace Mission in its literal sense: a refuge from a world that desperate souls had found unfulfilling and sometimes shattering.

Divine at first limited his role to blessing the first courses of food, a powerful ritual of communion described by a student of Harlem's religious cults, Arthur Huff Fauset:

> Every dish on which food is placed passes at least once through [Father Divine's] hands. When a platter of meat is to be sent around, Father Divine places the serving utensil upon the platter with his own hands. He places the ladle in the tureen of soup, he cuts the first slice of cake, pours the first glass of water, introduces the serving spoon into each container of ice cream. He is thus part of every activity of the feast.

Only after several hours had passed would Divine rise to preach. Even the minister's critics agreed that he was a master at moving crowds. Quick of mind and movement, he timed each banquet sermon to match the peak of popular clamor for his message. Then he rose "like a cat," in the words of one visitor, who compared Divine's instinct for an audience to the ringside skills of his contemporary, the ghetto-born boxing champion and national hero Joe Louis. The crowds cheered and Divine paused, "waiting, his eyes down and his arms hanging limp; the instant the last cheer has died, completely died, he comes alive, shoots out clipped words that fly like bullets."

In the manner of a southern black preacher, Divine encouraged shouted responses from the

crowds. He drew laughter with entertaining anec-
dotes and evoked "Amens" with stories of injustices
that touched many followers personally. To bring his
listeners into still fuller contact, he would follow up
a story or lesson with a phrase he made famous:
"Peace! It is truly wonderful!"

Individual sermons denounced racial prejudice,
called for moral conduct, and spoke of the unity and
harmony of all creatures. All his sermons spoke of
hope for mankind in this world and, most of all, for
the discouraged and downtrodden with him that
night. Father Divine told his listeners that all of them
had unlimited potential to do good, that they could
lead upstanding and prosperous lives without waiting
to go to Heaven in some distant place. He described
a society already coming, when all men and women
could view themselves as free and equal, as partakers
of the one, infinite spirit that created them.

Whether Divine preached 20 minutes or 2 hours,
one could see his followers intent to catch every word.
When he concluded with a modest "I thank you.
Peace!" the tightly massed disciples responded with
a roar of approval that to nervous outsiders seemed
never to end. Yet the service and celebration often
went on gaily, featuring further testimonies, singing,
dancing, and shouted praise without letup. This ritual
would be repeated with equal vigor and enthusiasm
the next day or perhaps in a matter of hours that same
evening.

Ecstasy reigned among the poor, the racially
outcast, and the troubled in spirit so long as the good
Father remained to inspire them. Twice a day, every
day, the banquets broke through the monotony of
their lives to bring them what they knew with deepest
belief was the kingdom of Heaven on earth. ❧

$$5$$

REFORM FROM WITHIN

FATHER DIVINE'S PERSONAL experience had convinced him that oppressed people had to take the first steps toward winning their own freedom. His own life showed that through pride, ambition, hard work, and a readiness to seize opportunities one could overcome the twin obstacles of prejudice and poverty. He therefore tried to instill these qualities in his disciples in the hope that they would rise from the slums and, through their example as model citizens, help reduce the racism that polluted society.

Father Divine wished to see his followers independent in both spirit and body. He warned them never to rely on state or private aid if they were able to work instead. He appealed to their often buried pride, explaining that "there is more respect for a person who can respect himself independently than that person who is dependent on charity."

Members of Divine's New York City congregation celebrate the chilly Easter of 1937 with a parade of praise for their leader. Such demonstrations received cordial assistance from the city's police, who appreciated the Peace Mission's tough approach to law and order. "I am for this little guy, Divine," said one admiring Manhattan detective.

Honesty became a watchword of the Peace Mission movement. Father Divine warned his followers, some of whom had once been criminals, that there was no such thing as a small or harmless theft: "He who would steal an apple would steal an elephant, if he could get him in his pocket, and get away with it, and he who would steal an egg would steal an ox, if he could get away with it."

Divine himself set a strict example of financial honesty for his disciples. Although he encouraged Peace Mission members to share their income, he returned all outside contributions, usually with a note "explaining" that God provided for his needs. He refused offers of $10,000 for speaking engagements on the grounds that it was wrong to charge for spreading the word of God. Unlike many cult leaders of the day, he denounced attempts to sell buttons and other items with his endorsement, calling it racketeering. Finally, he insisted that disciples spurn all government welfare that did not involve work, although this policy cost his movement a fortune. One local official estimated in 1939 that Divine's policy had saved New York City alone more than $2 million in welfare funds during the Great Depression.

Disciples literally matched their leader's honesty to the last dime. They sent stores both large and small payments for thefts committed in earlier, less pure states of being. One disciple astonished the head of the Central of Georgia Railway in the town of Macon by writing: "I wish to confess over forty years or more ago I rode the train from Andersonville, Georgia, to Americus, Georgia, without paying the fare. Since I have come in contact with Father Divine, he has caused me to confess and pay the same. Enclosed find 66 cents for the two rides."

That same week, a woman, who had perhaps recovered from the theft of some slippers 10 years earlier, received a letter from a former maid, Sallie

Jones, who said, "No doubt you'll be a bit surprised to hear from me. . . . I am sending you $2.50 to pay for a pair of mules of yours that was taken from Mrs. Cunningham's apartment."

The honesty of Father Divine's followers gained considerable respect for the movement. Outsiders may not have been converted by the return of a 75-cent debt, but they were frequently impressed, even overwhelmed, by the healthy impact Divine was making. A real estate agent named Fred Dickens expressed the feeling of many grateful merchants upon receiving payment for a bill long since given up as lost: "Then, I began to take Father Divine seriously."

Personal reform took discipline as well as good intentions, and Father Divine urged the avoidance of liquor and drugs. This had special importance to followers from the black ghettos, where crimes related

Nation of Islam chief Elijah Muhammad (center, behind microphones) addresses a 1966 Black Muslim rally in Chicago. Unlike Divine, who hoped to eliminate all racial barriers, Muhammad preached separatism and aimed his teachings exclusively at blacks. Both leaders, however, helped their disciples develop a strong sense of racial pride.

to alcoholism and drug addiction severely damaged the community. The Peace Mission centers banned all such "indulgences" and expelled anyone caught drinking or involved in a similar violation.

Contact with Father Divine inspired criminals to change their ways, and wherever new Peace Mission centers sprang up, the arrest rate fell. The reform of criminals by the Peace Mission was similar to the work of numerous sects and cults, such as the Nation of Islam, which offered its followers, known as Black Muslims, a sense of purpose and community. The Peace Mission, in addition, provided jobs to many who had formerly been unable to obtain respectable employment.

Some Peace Mission members contributed more actively to the fight against crime by warning dope peddlers to leave their neighborhoods. If a drug dealer refused, several of the larger, more muscular Angels would beat him and then alert police to where the dazed criminal could be found. Although it appeared to be a major exception to Father Divine's ideas on nonviolence, the minister actually encouraged this vigilante activity, declaring that if the mayor could not send enough police to arrest the criminals in Harlem, his own followers would clean up the neighborhoods.

The police, for their part, openly approved of such actions. "I wish all of Harlem belonged," a New York detective told a writer for the *Saturday Evening Post* in 1939. Another officer said, "I am for this little guy, Divine."

Among black leaders during the 1930s, no aspect of personal improvement received more attention than education. Whereas many black ghetto dwellers had attended segregated schools in the South that had left them largely illiterate, northern-born blacks were only slightly more fortunate to attend the inferior schools in Harlem, Newark, and other black areas. To make up for this, National Urban League executives and others in the black community helped organize special educational programs and urged adults to enroll in city night schools.

Father Divine reflected this concern for educating ghetto residents, and he applied his unique organizing talents to the task. When he preached for a return to public schools, his disciples responded in numbers that amazed the night-school administrators in New York City. Of 8,000 students enrolled in these schools in 1935, 98 percent were black, and about 20 percent, or 1,600 pupils, were followers of Father Divine. Among the celebrated cases of individual achievement by students from the Peace Mission was the work of Brother Joseph, who had left the third grade 80 years earlier but now returned to school at age 90. He explained, "There is always room to improve."

Father Divine's endless battles with racism deepened his concern for another group that suffered discrimination in the schools: the physically handicapped. Divine opposed the common practice of holding back and even denying graduation because of some physical disability. "This unjust condition exists in practically every community in the United States," he said, "but especially is it found in the school system of New York." This action could not be justified as a measure to save money, he wrote to the state education commissioner, because it was wrong to violate students' rights for reasons unrelated to their ability to learn.

Divine's emphasis on education reflected his view that learning was crucial to becoming good, useful citizens. This led him, for example, to call on colleges to welcome minority applicants more wholeheartedly. "Colleges that close their doors to any downtrodden people," he wrote, "are definitely breeders of immorality among men. They create unrest, and devitalize the energy and spirit of those who would advance themselves to become useful and profitable citizens of state and country."

Despite this belief in education, Father Divine warned his most learned disciples and guests never to look down on followers with less knowledge. A sincere spirit was still more important than formal learning. Remember, he said, God does not care about "the language of the saints, but [only] the meaning of their groans."

Divine was most concerned about the moral value of education. He believed that no truly learned person would be so prejudiced as to mistreat another because of his race or religious belief. No civilized society would permit discrimination to mar its laws and practices. Divine noted, as an example of empty study, those who recited and revered the Constitution yet did not support fully its principles of equal justice.

Divine leads his flock to the riverboat that will carry them to the Peace Mission's new property in Upstate New York. "It can certainly be said that of the various religious movements of our day, there is least in this that one may criticize," activist editor W. E. B. Du Bois wrote in the Harlem newspaper the Amsterdam News, "and as a social movement there can be no question but that it has helped many people who need help."

A journal called *Better Schools* invited Father Divine to explain his views on education in a column, "If I Were a College Professor." Divine wrote on the need for teachers to develop tolerance: "Real education consists of more than merely teaching men the subjects taught in a school curriculum. . . . I should eliminate all reference to races, creeds and colors from my classes . . . thus nipping in the bud, wars and race riots, vices and crimes, segregation and discrimination . . . in our educational system of today. . . . I would eliminate the very segregated terms referring to races, creeds and colors found in our books of learning, and I would teach men that 'of one blood God formed all nations.'"

All Father Divine's efforts to remold character found a common purpose in his desire to have whites and blacks mingle in harmony and equality. To accomplish this, he had to eliminate not only prejudice among whites but also the racial self-hatred that marked many black ghetto dwellers. Jim Crow barriers and poverty had long encouraged them to feel they were inferior. Before they could become fully independent and hardworking, they needed to throw off the racial shame that held them back. Toward this end, Divine tried to inspire followers to feel pride in their common humanity.

There was but one race, Father Divine insisted, and that was the human race. "A free people cannot be free," he said, "unless they are mentally and spiritually free from race superiority and race inferiority." Divine sought to end the use by newspapers of all racial terms, such as *Negro*, and did not even care for activities and awards for "Negro" or "colored" progress, for this still set people apart by race.

By the standards of a later generation of blacks accustomed to the proud assertion that black is beautiful, Father Divine's denial of race may appear

A unit of Peace Mission Angels heads up Lenox Avenue during a 1938 parade in New York City's Harlem. Many lay leaders within the black community disapproved of the cultlike enthusiasm of Divine's followers, yet they approved emphatically of his efforts to uplift the black masses socially, economically, politically, and even psychologically.

strange. Yet during the 1930s, when *Negro* more often than not was used to identify a segregated facility or a criminal, Divine's objections to the word were viewed as radical. Moreover, Divine discouraged the common practices among blacks in the 1930s of using hair straighteners and skin whiteners to look more like the dominant white population. No one, the minister said, should "try to make themselves altogether different from what they really are—my true followers do not do those things."

Father Divine's efforts to build strong, independent character helped many in the black ghettos reach undreamed-of levels of achievement. Those who once viewed their complexion as a crippling disadvantage, even a disgrace, now saw themselves as fully able, worthwhile individuals. Men and women who had never held steady employment or learned to read discovered that they could do these things and much more. Their potential had just been awakened.

At the same time, by aiding and uniting the most disadvantaged elements of black ghetto society, Father Divine reminded middle-class black Americans that racial justice depended on ending poverty and unemployment, not just Jim Crow practices. His ministry thus formed a distinctive part of the process by which black religious leaders became more boldly committed to the struggle for equality. It was a trend whose influence on race relations in America was to become ever more visible—and decisive—in succeeding decades. ❧

6

THE CHALLENGE TO SEGREGATION

·❦·

RACIAL INTEGRATION WAS the central theme of the Peace Mission's social program. Father Divine hoped that the movement's example of interracial harmony and equality would inspire the rest of American society. Instead, surrounding communities often resisted bitterly, and at times violently, the appearance of new Peace Mission branches precisely because these centers accepted blacks and whites together. Despite this opposition, the Peace Mission continued to spread its message of brotherhood in white as well as black neighborhoods.

The Peace Mission's approach to race relations was remarkable in an age when, even in the North, blacks were subject to separate and harshly unequal treatment. The vast majority lived in overcrowded ghettos and suffered discrimination by employers, unions, and even government aid programs. And although the North did not have Jim Crow laws like those in the South, northern blacks were still barred from many restaurants, hotels, resorts, and stores.

Divine receives a rousing welcome at Spencer's Point, the Upstate New York property he bought for the Peace Mission in 1938. The minister used the 500-acre estate—immediately dubbed "Divine Heaven" by the press—as a retreat for hardworking Mission members.

That the Peace Mission was a religious movement did not make its welcome of all people more
acceptable to the American public. This was a time
when more than 99 percent of congregations in the
North and South were either all white or all black.
Almost any white clergyman in the 1930s who dared
call for full racial integration risked his career.

As late as 1941, Edward Thomas McGuire, a
young white minister of the Church of God in Christ,
a sect that believed in racial equality, was arrested in
Memphis, Tennessee, as a public nuisance and held
incommunicado for two weeks. The city inspector
of Memphis justified this treatment by claiming
that McGuire "had been hanging around town all
hours of the night, frequenting Negro houses and
establishments and generally acting in a suspicious
manner." After the FBI cleared the minister of any
wrongdoing, the inspector ordered him released—
and expelled from the state. McGuire himself commented, "The real reason for my being treated so, I
believe, is because of my religious faith which pro-
motes racial equality. After I came to Memphis . . .
I conducted services in several Negro churches. At
some of them I preached to congregations which
included both Negroes and whites of our faith."

The boldness of the Peace Mission's stand on
integration is further highlighted by the absence
of almost any other black church or cult that
deliberately encouraged an interracial membership. Most black religious leaders preferred racial
separatism in the church because it protected
their authority and the independence of their
congregations.

In 1937, a leading black Baptist columnist, R. C.
Barbour, took Father Divine to task for daring to form
an integrated religious movement. "You are taking
Jesus too seriously in race matters," Barbour lectured
Divine in an open letter. "If you plan to preach in

America, do what we Baptists are doing, develop a jim-crow church. No-one will harm you then; and then, too, you can get by with anything."

Despite white opposition and black cautioning, Father Divine encouraged white membership in his movement. He also refused to limit his leadership to the black ghettos and instead set up Peace Mission branches in rich white suburbs, such as the Sutton Manor district of New Rochelle, New York, noted for its exclusive yacht clubs. In brief, Divine intended to foster nationwide integration as a way to overcome the roots of prejudice.

Divine moved swiftly but seldom directly to expand the Peace Mission's holdings in white neighborhoods during the 1930s and early 1940s.

As he tours Spencer's Point in Krum Elbow, New York, Divine points with amusement to the misspelled sign at its gate. He considered such lapses immaterial: God, he maintained, was concerned with good hearts, not good grammar.

In order to get around agreements among white homeowners and real estate agents never to sell to blacks (known as restrictive housing covenants), he had white followers arrange purchases for the movement. They often added to the deed of sale the names of black as well as white followers of Father Divine but made no mention of the minister or that the property would henceforth have an interracial ownership. After the sale, Divine often arrived to oversee the "housewarming" ceremonies with a racially mixed group, to the surprise and often dismay of the surrounding residents.

This preference for secrecy extended even to the purchase of a building located on the edge of Harlem. In 1938, Frank Warner paid $24,000 for a 50-room mansion on Madison Avenue. The owner, a white physician, had no notion that Warner was a follower of Divine's and that his home had been chosen as a

Divine's guests explore the spacious house and 500-acre lawn of Spencer's Point. The evangelist's purchase of the estate opened the area to black people, traditionally strangers to New York State's beautiful rolling countryside.

private residence for the Peace Mission leader, his 12 secretaries, and a few chosen disciples.

Only some weeks after the contract had been signed did Father Divine appear at the home to introduce himself and request permission to look the place over. "I was astounded," said the owner. He gave Divine a full tour while Divine peppered him with questions and remarks such as "It's wonderful." The overwhelmed physician acknowledged, "I never saw anything like it."

If Divine's mode of operations might appear overly secretive today, it reflected the reality of his day that blacks were almost never permitted to buy homes in white neighborhoods even if they could afford them. Indeed, even after Peace Mission members managed to obtain properties near white-owned homes, they often faced danger from prejudiced neighbors. In Colorado Springs, Colorado, white vigilantes surrounded a Peace Mission church, poured gasoline in the street, and tossed a lighted match on the gasoline, while someone in the crowd hurled a rock through a window of the church. Colorado's governor at first refused to protect the Peace Mission members, while an aide ordered them to leave their church, thus encouraging the mob.

Police in some states sometimes actively persecuted Peace Mission members in order to maintain segregation. In Florida, police imprisoned Peace Mission disciples, and one officer threatened, "You ought to be hung, you will never get out of here." Private extremist groups also opposed the Peace Mission's activities. The Ku Klux Klan handed out leaflets in New York City, denouncing Father Divine and warning that "overtolerance" had permitted matters to get out of hand.

With his shrewd sense of symbolism, Divine had much the better of his propaganda fight with the Ku Klux Klan. In 1934, he personally negotiated the purchase of an estate in Ulster County, New York. Among the oldest homes in the United States, it had once been a base from which Klan members rode on cross-burning missions to terrorize blacks. Under Divine's new direction, the home became the headquarters for a series of interracial rural communities he established to the northwest of New York City, known to his followers as the Promised Land.

The Peace Mission frequently chose properties at least partly for their value in dramatizing the cause of interracial harmony. The outstanding example was Divine's purchase, in 1938, of Spencer's Point, an estate across the Hudson River from President Franklin D. Roosevelt's mansion in Hyde Park, New York. By this act of public relations genius, the Father and his interracial following became known as the president's neighbors while also gaining a luxurious 500-acre property.

Roosevelt himself, already attacked by southern congressmen who believed he was too sympathetic to the cause of black rights, tried to avoid comment about Father Divine's purchase. Divine therefore wrote the president and his wife, Eleanor, asking their views on his movement's intent to purchase another nearby property. Both replied—Eleanor Roosevelt personally and the president through his press secretary—expressing their belief that any citizen should be able to acquire whatever property he desired.

Divine immediately made their correspondence public. He later explained, "[Many have said], 'If President Roosevelt can be his neighbor, why not I?' . . . I believe that has curbed a whole lot of antagonism." Divine added an understandably pleased afterthought: "And I am always thinking of something like that, you know."

The Peace Mission often acquired properties in order to challenge specific racial injustices, such as

the barring of blacks from beaches and pools. This exclusion was a source of racial friction throughout the early 20th century. Blacks and whites both saw the practice as symbolic of broader efforts to deny social equality to black Americans. The violence at a Chicago beach, triggering that city's massive race riot in 1919, was one of many similar incidents that occurred in large urban centers.

New Jersey, with many resort areas, was a major offender in the treatment of black vacationers. In Long Branch, for example, black bathers coming from all sections of the state to enjoy the July Fourth holiday in 1939 were forbidden to use the best beaches because they were "for white people." This was the general situation Father Divine sought to

As a pair of immense Hudson River steamers await the return to New York City of Divine and his 2,500 guests, the group follows its leader around Spencer's Point. Divine liked to point out that across the river was Hyde Park, the country residence of President Franklin D. Roosevelt and his family.

remedy when, in 1942, he supervised the purchase of the main hotel in Brigantine, New Jersey, together with rights to its excellent beaches and boardwalk near Atlantic City.

The acquiring of this choice property bore the hallmark of Divine's distinctive methods. He selected a site of considerable value, but his followers paid a relatively modest price for it—in this case, $75,000 for a 154-room, 154-bath 10-story building on a luxury island facing Atlantic City's famed boardwalk. The hotel was easily the most prominent building in Brigantine and could be seen from a distance of five miles. White intermediaries made the purchase, all the while in secret consultation with Father Divine. Brigantine officials connected with the sale first learned of the Peace Mission's interest in the purchase only after the contract had been signed and Divine had arrived to inspect the premises.

The influx of black as well as white followers outraged the residents of the isle. With virtually one voice, they demanded that the Peace Mission members resell their hotel to the city. The conflict that followed between the new owners and the townspeople of Brigantine showed Father Divine at his most ingenious and American racism at its most vicious.

A mass meeting of the island's residents began the hostilities. A town councilman spoke against Father Divine's move, and some islanders threatened to rip up the boardwalk in front of the hotel. Divine, wearily familiar with such receptions, said simply that his followers would build a connection of some kind to their private pier. Shortly afterward, the councilman formally objected to the presence of Divine and his interracial following as harmful to property values in Brigantine.

Brigantine's mayor, Vincent Haneman, who feared an explosion of racial violence if the townspeople were not quickly satisfied, headed a delegation to persuade Father Divine to sell back the property. The mayor assured the minister that he personally was not prejudiced but added that not everyone was so progressive in these matters. It was therefore necessary for Father Divine to withdraw his followers at a fair price for the good of all concerned. The mayor concluded, "What we are talking about is practical results . . . whether [remaining here] will not defeat the ends that you [and I] are trying to obtain." He believed that Divine would surely agree to such "reasonable" appeals, but he could not have been more mistaken.

"Well, positively not!" Divine cut off the mayor's speech on the virtues of surrendering to racial prejudice. This was a time to put basic issues of human dignity to the test. Divine suggested that the mayor should let the residents of Brigantine "know of your personal contact [with Peace Mission members] and let them know we are not idiots" or "just out of the wild woods, as lots of people may think—we have the most refined people."

No agreement was reached, so the town government pressured the Peace Mission to resell the property by threatening new taxes on the hotel and beachfront, amounting to a fine of more than $60,000. Father Divine countered with a wholly unexpected maneuver; at a time when Coast Guard units in the area were desperately short of housing, Divine asked his followers to donate use of the hotel to the Coast Guard. This patriotic gesture sparked positive news coverage of Divine's presence in Brigantine and created pressure on the city government to abandon the proposed tax increases.

Yet if Brigantine officials had not counted on Divine's cunning, he in turn underestimated the strength of Brigantine's racial prejudice. After a period of confusion, Brigantine's representatives enacted a 400 percent tax increase on the Peace Mission's property.

At last, seeing race madness worsening, Father Divine counseled his followers to sell their property. But he had one more surprise for the island of Brigantine. The new owner, a wealthy cosmetics executive named Sara Washington (who paid the nominal sum of $1), was a black woman and frequent visitor at the main Peace Mission center in Harlem.

The struggle between Father Divine and Brigantine had resembled a contest between an irresistible principle and an immovable prejudice, and the verdict was mixed. Some observers, noting the caution of Brigantine's politicians in the face of racial prejudice, the huge financial loss to the Peace Mission, and the followers' withdrawal from Brigantine, saw the episode as a setback for Father Divine and the cause of toleration in general.

Still, Father Divine was among the first to provide an integrated beachfront in the area of Atlantic City, and if this achievement was short-lived, it still helped encourage the broader movement for racial integration. The NAACP, for example, monitored the Brigantine incident and rejoiced to see Divine

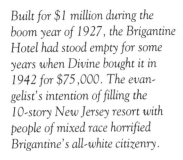

Built for $1 million during the boom year of 1927, the Brigantine Hotel had stood empty for some years when Divine bought it in 1942 for $75,000. The evangelist's intention of filling the 10-story New Jersey resort with people of mixed race horrified Brigantine's all-white citizenry.

defy long-standing bigotry on that island. An NAACP official praised Divine in 1942 for his "masterful" argument to the Brigantine committees and his "courageous attitude" in confronting those "un-American" citizens who barred the path to full justice for all.

In reply, Father Divine emphasized the larger social aims that motivated all his actions: "My co-workers and followers . . . mean to protect the civil liberties of the law-abiding American citizens in every community and give them a chance to enjoy some of the pleasures and liberties that [only] the privileged few [could] enjoy."

On balance, Father Divine's campaign to integrate even the most exclusive northern white neighborhoods enjoyed significant positive results. It is true that the severe racism in the country limited the Peace Mission's efforts to enter new communities and change national attitudes. Yet despite frustrations in Brigantine and elsewhere, followers who had known only segregated slums were enabled to acquire homes in excellent residential areas once barred to them. The movement's purchases also showed white Americans that blacks would vigorously test their constitutional rights to live wherever they could afford to.

Perhaps most important, the Peace Mission inspired blacks within and outside the movement to realize that through their determined efforts they could make the ghettos into points of departure for a better life. ❧

7

A NEW ECONOMIC ORDER

ALTHOUGH FATHER DIVINE considered integration essential to racial harmony, he believed that equal rights also had to include economic opportunity. Although he is remembered largely for feeding and housing the poor during the Depression, he in fact disliked the idea of welfare and considered it degrading to those who received it and a burden to society. He viewed his charitable work as a necessary humanitarian activity but only a temporary solution. His long-range economic plan was to bring prosperity for everyone through economic cooperation.

The cooperative ideal that Father Divine set forth, in which a community completely shared resources, business ownership, and profits, was already gaining favor among some black leaders. This idea offered, first, a way to reduce consumer costs and raise the efficiency of black-owned businesses. It also appealed to many in the black community as a way to bring racial solidarity through mutual economic aid.

Peace Mission members buy U.S. War Bonds in 1944. Because most of Divine's flock used unconventional names—this group, for example, included Mr. Eve Love, Mr. Seven Stars, Miss Faithful Child, and Miss Wonderful Sincere—Treasury officials were at first reluctant to sell them bonds; the sight of $94,000 in hard cash, however, persuaded the officials to make the transaction.

Father Divine's distinctive contribution lay in proving, through his organizing genius, that voluntary economic cooperation could succeed on a large scale.

The Peace Mission was among the most impressive examples of cooperative enterprise in the nation. By the mid-1930s, the Peace Mission had become the largest landholder in Harlem, with 3 apartment houses, 9 private houses, 15 to 20 flats, and several meeting halls with dormitories on the upper floors. In addition, followers in Harlem operated some 25 restaurants, 6 groceries, 10 barbershops, 10 cleaning stores, 2 dozen huckster wagons with clams and oysters or fresh vegetables, and a coal business with 3 trucks ranging from Harlem to the mines in Pennsylvania. Divine's aide, Faithful Mary, alone directed over a dozen such businesses in 1935, among them a large market for meat, fish, fowl, and vegetables, an ice cream and bakery store, and a tailor shop. A variety of Peace Mission businesses also operated in other areas, from New England to California.

Father Divine encouraged his followers to enter business as a sign of their independence. The response was remarkable. Hundreds with little experience enthusiastically became merchants. Most returned their profits to the common funds of the Peace Mission, relying on Father Divine to provide for their needs. Similarly, some followers volunteered to work for others who had established businesses, yet they received no wages except to cover transportation and other expenses related to their jobs.

Individual merchants displaying Peace buttons were a common sight near Father Divine's main centers. Typically, they built up healthy trades from extremely modest beginnings, as a visitor to Harlem observed of one pushcart merchant serving up frozen desserts: "He has a block of ice, some sort of metal shaver, and with this he scrapes the shavings into a

Manhattan shoppers stroll past Father Divine's Delicatessen, Grocery, and Vegetable Store, one of dozens of businesses operated by the Peace Mission in the 1930s and 1940s. Profits from this and similar enterprises helped pay for the Mission's extensive free-food program.

cup, pours on the various colored syrups which he has in bottles, and there is your ice! These are sold for the trifling sum of three cents. Quite ingenious, the way some of the believers have succeeded in making themselves practical and independent."

How did the Peace Mission businesses do so well during the Depression, when businesses all around them were failing? The nature of the religious movement itself helped greatly, beginning with the communal living arrangements. Followers saved money by living snugly in large buildings, which were typically purchased at reduced cost during this time of falling prices. Bulk purchases helped the Peace Mission win discounted prices for food and other necessities. The movement also had no expenses for such forbidden products as tobacco, liquor, cosmetics, and other common but costly pleasures. It was therefore relatively easy for Peace Mission businesses, together with wages from outside work, to meet the basic needs of the members and still provide ample funds for investments in property or starting new economic ventures.

These businesses succeeded, too, because Divine avoided a mistake often fatal to black-owned businesses: dependence on racial solidarity for patronage. Indeed, the sad record of such businesses during this period suggests that many blacks preferred to deal with white merchants whose chain stores undersold small black-operated shops and whose large banks were considered sounder than smaller, minority-owned banks.

Father Divine encouraged his disciples to seek customers for their businesses by offering economic advantages rather than racial appeals. Although he left details to the members, he urged them to keep prices low. His sermons recalled the Puritans' view of business as a calling from God to serve people. "Do not go in business for the purpose of seeing how much you will gain," he said, "but go in it to see how much you can give." This, he assured his followers, "will give you a desirable result." He cited the example of the manufacturer and national hero Henry Ford, who built better—and cheaper—cars than his competition and sold so many that he became one of the world's richest men.

Under Divine's guidance, Peace Mission members sold quality goods at fire-sale prices, taking advantage of the movement's low cost of living and relying on sheer volume of trade to bring in large revenues. Peace Mision coal vendors charged $7.50 a ton in 1935, a full dollar below the regular market price. Peace Mission restaurants gained national fame for selling complete and nourishing meals for 15 cents, a price lower than almost anywhere else in Harlem. Lodgings, too, were inexpensive at one to two dollars a week; if rooms were often crowded, a comparison with most other dwellings in the same neighborhood left little cause for complaint.

Although some competing merchants criticized the Peace Mission for unfair pricing policies, shoppers took a rather different view. Divine's followers did a thriving trade with customers whose only interest in the movement was an appreciation for low-priced

About to close a real estate deal in a Newark, New Jersey, bank, a Peace Mission officer rests his feet on a batch of cash-filled suitcases. Divine and his followers often amazed bankers by showing up, unarmed and unguarded, with huge sums of currency. These bags held half a million dollars, which took 14 tellers almost 4 hours to count.

goods. Given the high cost of living in the ghettos, these stores provided a crucial service during the Depression by helping hard-pressed workers make ends meet.

The possibilities of rural cooperatives intrigued Father Divine, for they served important social as well as economic needs. Many of his followers had found it difficult to adjust to urban life. This was particularly true of those who had only recently migrated from the rural South and who longed for at least some features of their old routine instead of crammed city tenements. For such people, the Peace Mission offered the chance to resume a rural life on properties it purchased in New York's Ulster County. These new farm settlements became known to Divine's faithful as the Promised Land.

Various land-oriented schemes of this nature, such as Marcus Garvey's back-to-Africa dream in the 1920s, had arisen throughout black American history, but few had proved practical. Father Divine's resettlement project was in some ways less ambitious but far more successful. Instead of a return to Africa, which seldom appealed to black Americans except as a spur to racial pride, Divine directed the investment of cooperative funds in rich farmland a few hours from his Harlem centers. He told his followers, "If you have the means to build a home, [then] the ground, the land, the lots, will be given to you free of cost, and you will have your deeds for them without a string tied to them. All the property I have purchased is free and clear."

Thousands became joint owners in these co-operative communities, each receiving small lots of land between 5 and 10 acres. Those who worked in factories and offices could choose between communal homes and modest private residences. The communities soon began to produce fruits, vegetables, poultry, and eventually—with some thought to biblical symbolism—milk and honey.

Followers often arranged the land purchases themselves but usually checked with Father Divine and asked his advice on the best real estate values. The Father seemed to have spent much time consulting with legal aides and others in selecting the best sites and the wisest bargains. He also had the comfortable advantage of having real estate agents come to him with offers in all parts of New York. They knew he paid cash for all deals, no matter the price, and always in advance.

Armed with this financial clout and a shrewd business sense, Divine often negotiated deals personally. He was reported to drive sharp bargains and to study every detail of a property before agreeing to buy it. When satisfied, he sealed a contract with a single cash payment from a brown bag or satchel bursting with paper currency. This money represented part of the pooled savings of his followers. The deeds were always in the names of his disciples, never his own.

Throughout Ulster County, the Peace Mission spurred economic growth that benefited entire communities, such as the village of High Falls, which had been in economic decline until Peace Mission followers settled there in the mid-1930s. A reporter found that Father Divine's disciples turned the town around:

> They moved in and bought up some of the best property in Ulster County. Today a flourishing shoe repair shop, a barber shop, a dress-making concern where fine women's clothes are made; and a second-hand clothing store where sterilized used clothing is sold, are operating full blast. Divine's restaurant does more business than any eating place in the village. His tailoring shop is considered the largest custom-made tailoring establishment in the entire county. A grocery store does the major business in the village.

Although High Falls's white residents grumbled at first that the Peace Mission's interracial following would destroy property values, they soon discovered a very different trend. As in other villages, it was observed, "homes and buildings were renovated throughout and the example set by Divine's faithful launched a community-wide campaign for similar improvement. Property values, real-estate men reported, have increased and police said no disorders of any kind have come up in the Divine communities."

White racism quickly faded as longtime residents enjoyed the economic benefits that Peace Mission settlers brought as merchants, servants, home renovators, and simply law-abiding citizens. "Those fellows who follow Father Divine don't do anyone harm," a white farmer in Ulster County said. "They're down there in High Falls doing something worthwhile."

Father Divine delighted in the progress made by hardworking settlers on these farms. Once, after looking over a colossal 62-pound pumpkin, he gleefully reported to his Harlem followers, "The vegetable kingdom is willingly surrendering." He saw in the abundant harvests a blessing for so many of the nation's poor: "I would like all of you to see all of" the "chickens and ducks and guineas and pigs and horses and cows and everything! It is just marvelous to see what God has actually done, for the meek and the most insignificant, they are coming into possession of their rightful inheritance and shall no longer be in lacks, wants and limitations and in the slums and dirt and filth."

Father Divine's vision of change surprisingly did not include a role for the labor unions that were springing up during the 1930s, aided by federal laws. Divine strongly discouraged disciples from joining unions, which he said pressured workers unfairly (and at times violently) into joining and conducting strikes. His views had some truth, but they ignored the crucial role of unions in lifting workers from poverty, brutal factory conditions, 70-hour work weeks, and nearly total helplessness. During the Depression, organized labor was winning some of its

A Harlem shoeshine parlor, like other Mission businesses, offers a hard-to-match bargain: a three-cent shoeshine (but no tips and no smoking). Tolerant of many human failings, Divine was absolutely opposed to smoking, drinking, and drug use, any of which could get a member expelled.

greatest battles, yet Father Divine for the most part remained a cold critic from the sidelines.

Divine's hostility toward unions was at odds with his enthusiasm for many other forms of interracial cooperation. But it typified the attitudes of many black leaders, stemming from a history of racial discrimination by organized labor. During the early 20th century, most unions excluded blacks. In addition, white union members often beat up black strikebreakers, or scabs, who were often unable to get work in an industry under any other circumstances. These blacks usually accepted jobs unaware of raging labor conflicts and were caught between two cynical parties: white workers trying to keep them out of an industry and white businessmen employing them for low wages to weaken union pressures.

Although unions in rising industries, such as the United Auto Workers, were starting to recruit blacks on a basis of relative equality during the Depression, the signs of racism within many older, elite craft unions were still clearly visible. Only in the late 1930s did unionism become more a help than a hindrance to black workers. Yet even then, Father Divine continued to treat these organizations as if they were Devil-sent rivals for control of his followers.

Whatever the limits to Divine's reform vision, his practical achievements in a time of general economic catastrophe were singular. There was, of course, his well-known charitable work for thousands of poor people. His programs also provided employment, training, and business opportunities for ghetto residents, supported by a hugely successful and rapidly growing cooperative movement. In such ways, the Peace Mission helped its members not only to survive in the ghettos but to challenge the basic economic conditions that had confined them. ❧

8

THE POLITICS OF RACIAL JUSTICE

❧

THE DESIRE TO make basic changes in race relations increasingly drew Father Divine into politics. Unlike some black cult leaders, such as Elijah Muhammad of the Black Muslims, who rejected all white institutions, Divine believed deeply in American political ideals and processes. Moreover, unlike many black clergymen, who tended to avoid controversial political protests, he insisted that the struggle for justice was the highest religious calling.

The Peace Mission exerted its greatest influence in Harlem, where blacks were already organizing more boldly in defense of common racial interests. To help combat discrimination against blacks in local politics, Divine supported local coalitions spanning a range of community groups and political beliefs. There was, for example, the All People's Party, which Father Divine helped found in 1936. Composed of 89 groups, including 5 religious bodies, the All People's Party called for government measures to bring full employment at decent wages and to lower rents for ghetto dwellers.

Political reform on their minds, Peace Mission members march through Harlem in the late 1930s. Divine, who opened his crusade for "Righteous Government" in 1936, called for improved universal education and the elimination of lynching, segregation, unemployment, capital punishment, and war.

Eight of the nine so-called Scottsboro Boys line up for a jailhouse photograph in 1937, six years after they were sentenced to death for raping two young white women near Scottsboro, Alabama. Divine and many others, white and black, had vigorously campaigned for justice in this whirlwind case in which the incriminating evidence was extremely weak.

Although many black ministers disliked Father Divine's cult leadership, they were sometimes willing to overlook their differences in order to work for common political aims, such as campaigns to rescue individual victims of racial injustice. The most famous of these involved the so-called Scottsboro Boys, nine black youths convicted in Alabama, on doubtful evidence, of having raped two young white women. The blatant racism of the court trials, in which eight of the youths were sentenced to death, illustrated what the civil rights leader, scholar, and visionary W. E. B. Du Bois once called a "judicial lynching." Although the efforts to aid the Scottsboro Boys eased their lot only to a limited degree, they did much to impress on the nation the evils of a Jim Crow system that had subjected nine bewildered and probably innocent youths to years in prison, public degradation, and mortal danger.

Father Divine was among the outspoken supporters of the Scottsboro Boys in sermons, interviews, and letters. His strong statements and ability to stir mass action led Thomas H. Harten of New York's Holy Trinity Baptist Church, normally a bitter critic of all cult leaders, to join Father Divine at a rally to raise money for the Scottsboro prisoners and dramatize their plight. Both ministers explained to the audience that personal and religious differences were unimportant to them so long as they could contribute to the cause of racial justice.

Father Divine's varied ideas for overcoming social injustice in America found their most complete expression at a three-day convention of his disciples in January 1936. Six thousand followers, including many from California and several from Europe, gathered in Harlem's Rockland Palace to endorse and expand Father Divine's new political testament. The document that emerged from these proceedings, hailed as a "Righteous Government Platform" by Peace Mission members, aimed to create full equality of opportunity, undisturbed by race prejudice or violence.

Divine dominated the meeting. He proposed most planks, guided the procedure, and even led the wild applause that greeted his own declarations. A follower's declaration that Father Divine was God on earth brought unanimous cheering from the delegates. In spite of this glorification of one man, the Peace Mission assembly seriously addressed difficult issues of justice and social planning. Challenges from segregation to unemployment received detailed analysis and equally detailed plans to remedy them.

Ten of the 14 introductory planks in the Righteous Government Platform sought to correct racial inequalities. In an era when segregation in American life was seldom challenged, the most important of these planks called for sweeping civil rights legislation "making it a crime to discriminate in any public place against any individual on account of race, creed, or color, abolishing all segregated neighborhoods in cities and towns, making it a crime for landlords or hotels to refuse tenants on such grounds; abolishing all segregated schools and colleges, and all segregated areas in churches, theatres, public conveyances, and other public areas."

As befitted an organization whose mission was peace, the Righteous Government Platform contained proposals to foster nonviolence. One plank called for an end to capital punishment, another appealed to all nations to abolish the weapons of war, and a third called on the U.S. government in particular to put an end to lynching.

A section on economic reform focused on the goal of ending poverty and unemployment—if possible, through private business, but if necessary through direct government efforts to provide each adult with a well-paying job. No person should be left out of America's prosperity, for, in Divine's words, "The spectacle of hungry people in a land of plenty is worse than uncivilized."

The concluding section of the document focused on education. It called for free schooling for every child, banning school texts that glorified war or promoted racial superiority, and proposed instituting "Peace!" as a standard greeting to remind citizens of the evils of war for generations to come. The section thus captured the essence of the entire document—equal opportunity, racial harmony, and nonviolence.

Like most plans to perfect society, the Righteous Government Platform revealed significant problems.

Its many proposals for change were given no clear order of priorities, nor was it clear whether the society would be capitalist or socialist (apart from voluntary cooperation). These limitations, however serious, were not uncommon in the Depression decade of the 1930s, which saw a great deal of confusion in and outside government about just how to help set the economy on its feet again. Reform proposals, often contradictory, emerged from many sources, all groping for ways to help the poor and to ensure future prosperity.

A more serious political difficulty of the Righteous Government convention was its cele-bration of Father Divine as God, which naturally tended to drive away many people who otherwise approved of his political stands. The convention's

Peace Mission disciples attempt to place themselves on the Philadelphia voting lists in 1946. Divine encouraged his followers to claim their voting rights, but their efforts were often frustrated by election officials who refused to recognize their religious names.

direct influence on American politics was therefore minimal.

Despite these limitations, the Righteous Government Platform was important for its insight into the needs of the poor and minorities and for recognizing the potential of helpful federal action. Like the best reform documents, it anticipated much of government policy and concern over subsequent decades. Many of its proposals, later championed independently by other groups, became part of federal programs in civil rights, aid to education, and other areas. In particular, the concept of federal responsibility for ensuring desegregation and full employment appeared in far bolder form in this Peace Mission document than in government circles for decades afterward.

The major immediate accomplishment of the Righteous Government convention was to strengthen the Peace Mission's various lobbying efforts for civil rights. First, it signaled that Father Divine and his followers would henceforth play an active role in national politics. At the same time, the document provided a basic philosophy for the marches, petition campaigns, and other activities in which Peace Mission members engaged.

Divine's political efforts focused mainly on aid to the growing campaign for a federal antilynching law. Such bills had been proposed in Congress since 1919, at the strong initiative of the NAACP, only to be stopped by southern filibusters, which buried the bill in endless debate until its defenders gave up trying to pass it.

During the 1930s, many civil rights leaders emphasized the antilynching issue even more than employment, housing, and other matters of immediate importance to black Americans because it was the most dramatic example of racism at its most lawless. A federal antilynching bill enjoyed wide public support, and even in the South there was increasing opposition to mob violence. Civil rights leaders, particularly in the NAACP, believed that a triumph by antilynching forces would give new vigor and morale to many other campaigns against racism.

Father Divine grasped the symbolic value of the NAACP's battle against lynching, seeing in it a higher contest between the forces of law and justice and those of passion and prejudice. He did not believe that an antilynching law would actually do much to stop lynchings—that would require changing "the minds and hearts and lives of the people," which, he said, "will do more overnight" than a law would do in years. Still, the bill should be passed "so that we will go on record as a nation refusing to endorse lynching, or murder, without due process of law, which is not according to the Constitution."

Divine worked vigorously to impress on his followers the importance of the antilynching campaign, infusing it with both spiritual and political qualities. He preached, with a fervor possibly stemming from personal experience, that lynching represented the opposite of the Peace Mission's central goal of "eradicating prejudice, segregation, and division from among the people." At the banquet tables, psalms of praise mingled with antilynching songs that envisioned an America freed from racial violence.

Father Divine and his aides drafted a sample bill in 1936 and had it introduced later in Congress by a representative from Westchester, New York. It was stronger than the bills then being discussed in the Senate and in the House of Representatives and showed how much more could be done to deter lynchings. Divine's model bill required that every member of a lynch mob be tried, not just the leaders, and that, if convicted, they should be sentenced as if for first-degree murder no matter what the motives involved. And like the strongest congressional proposals, Divine's bill also insisted on a minimum $10,000 fine on any county in which the sheriff or other officials allowed a lynching to occur. The money was to compensate families of lynching victims.

The Peace Mission's activity did not escape notice of the Senate's veteran filibusterer against antilynching bills, Allen Ellender of Louisiana. On the Senate floor, Ellender linked his denunciations of a federal antilynching bill to Father Divine's influence in Harlem, which he viewed as a threat to the southern way of life. The senator ridiculed the worship of Divine—for racial rather than religious reasons—saying, "Imagine a people believing that the son of a slave is God!" Ellender urged measures to deny blacks the right to vote because people such as Father Divine, who enjoyed local political influence, were spreading "social equality" regardless of color.

In Washington, D.C., in 1940, Divine presents a stack of petitions to Robert Callahan, an aide of New York senator Robert Wagner's. Divine, who considered wholehearted political activity essential for all citizens, often sponsored petition drives to keep legislators informed of their constituents' desires: This batch urged the United States to unite with the governments of South America to create "everlasting peace."

The defeat of an antilynching bill in 1938 prompted its supporters to introduce a similar bill in 1940 and to press for it with even greater urgency. Divine's followers again contributed: In New York alone, the disciples gathered a quarter of a million signatures on copies of a petition urging immediate passage of the bill. Many followers accompanied Divine to Washington, D.C., to present the petition to key senators. Unknown to these pilgrims, however, Congress had adjourned. For Divine, the keenest disappointment may actually have been the absence of Allen Ellender, whose office he made it a point to visit.

The 1940 bill also fell to a southern filibuster, but the campaign held long-range benefits to the civil rights cause. It brought issues of racial justice closer to the center of public attention and led some southern states to pass their own measures against lynching in order to lessen pressure for a national bill. The campaign also acted as a testing ground for the movement, which gained valuable experience for later efforts to enact civil rights laws.

Father Divine aided this process by providing an outlet for poor blacks to express their resentments against lynching and racism in constructive political ways: as petitioners, marchers, and Washington lobbyists. If the techniques they and other civil rights workers used were often unpolished and neglected, they were still gathering force for campaigns and victories to come.

Father Divine's greatest limitation as a political activist was his small influence over elections. In part, this was because prejudiced registrars often blocked the registration of Divine's followers on the weak excuse that disciples who had taken spiritual names such as Happy Lamb and John Love could not legally use such names for voting. Apart from these questionable tactics (later ruled illegal obstruction of voting by a New York appeals court), Divine seemed to prefer an outsider's role toward both major political parties. Thus, he often criticized politicians for caution on civil rights issues and seldom endorsed anyone for office. In 1936, when both major party candidates for president refused to back an anti-lynching bill, Father Divine ordered his followers to stay home rather than vote for either. But this directive failed to prevent President Franklin D. Roosevelt from winning overwhelmingly, in Harlem as in the nation generally.

Divine enjoyed significantly greater impact as a political educator, a role more suited to his evangelical temperament. Many of his followers had spent decades in the South, where political activity and knowledge were considered reserved for whites. It required all of Divine's effort to give these people a sense of political awareness and interest.

In his sermons, Father Divine acknowledged that some might think it "absurd" for a minister of God to place such importance on political activity. He answered that the whole point of his leadership was to free people from their oppressions. And to do that he had first to make them realize what they wanted deep down inside: "You know you want your emancipation, you know you want your constitutional rights, you know you want social equality, you know you want religious liberty, you know you want health and happiness, and you know positively well you also want a chance to earn a living, the same as everybody else. That is what I came for."

The Peace Mission by 1933 made political education a part of its activities. State and local officials regularly lectured to Peace Mission gatherings about current political issues and how government worked in the United States. Divine also organized formal classes on basic political science within the Peace Mission centers. The class, called "U.S.A.," for example, taught "Americanism," citizenship, and government and required students to study the Declaration of Independence and the Constitution.

The reason for this careful attention to American political documents was revealed by a young member of the Peace Mission, who described her old, segregated school in Georgia this way: "The [white] school had a course called 'civics.' We didn't, though. We had one called 'character building.'" While the white children learned about the Constitution, "we learned what they called 'courtesy' and 'humility.'"

Divine, possibly remembering the effects of his own scant education in the South, was determined to spare his followers the same enforced ignorance and timidity. He wished to give people a sense, for the first time, that they could play an active role in shaping their destinies and the character of their society. In this he touched many lives, marking, perhaps, the real height of his political career. ❦

9

FROM CULT TO CORPORATION

◆◆◆

THE PEACE MISSION evolved after 1940 from a mass movement wholly dependent on its founding father to a formal religious sect with a large bureaucracy. Such trends are typical of charismatic movements after the passing of the original leader; but here the Peace Mission was transformed while Father Divine still lived and firmly controlled its affairs. Under the pressures of advancing age and growing legal problems, he tried to build permanent guarantees for the movement that he had once maintained through sheer charisma, energy, and seemingly endless ingenuity.

The occasion spurring the Peace Mission's change was a bitter court fight spanning more than five years and exposing a vulnerable side to the movement's legal and financial status. A former follower, Verinda Brown, sued in 1937 for money she claimed she had given to Father Divine in trust while a disciple. On the face of it, Brown had a dubious case: She had no direct evidence, she had obviously enjoyed many

Loyalists shower Divine with confetti as he announces his move to Philadelphia in 1942. When former disciple Verinda Brown won a lawsuit against him, the evangelist had seemingly faced only two choices: pay Brown the money she claimed he owed her or go to jail. Resourceful as ever, Divine created a third choice by simply removing himself from the reach of the New York courts.

material benefits while a Peace Mission member for five years, and she fairly admitted that Father Divine had never directly solicited anything from her. Yet a New York court ruled against Divine, placing the burden of proof on him and implicitly viewing his leadership as outside the full protection of the law.

The court's judgment of about $7,000 was a trivial sum by the standards of Peace Mission finance, but Father Divine realized that payment would only tempt other discontented or greedy disciples to file similar suits. As each of several appeals courts upheld the decision, the weary cult leader prepared drastic action to ensure his personal freedom and the security of his kingdom.

In 1941, Father Divine incorporated several key Peace Mission centers in the Northeast. This marked a decisive break with his earlier stress on an "invisible" church that was not dependent on legal records. Yet this new policy offered Divine's movement important legal advantages. It gave the Peace Mission legal status on a par with other churches, providing at least some defense against trial judges who tended to treat the Peace Mission as a barely legitimate "racket." Incorporation also allowed each official church to deed property in its own name so that no disciples could claim any of the movement's assets on leaving the Peace Mission, as Verinda Brown was attempting to do.

Unlike the Righteous Government Platform of 1936, which consisted of several dozen proposals for improving the country and the world, the Peace Mission's new document—its corporate bylaws—treated only the running of the Peace Mission itself. For the first time, Father Divine formally recognized a leadership class of Peace Mission officers who would govern the various churches. For years, Divine had avoided creating official groups that would set some members above others. But the needs of the movement in "middle age" set limits on efforts to maintain equality among all members.

The corporate charter's bylaws also formally stated the absolute leadership role of Father Divine. In earlier years, he had declined any special rank despite the reverence that his followers displayed toward him. He was, in the polite fiction of his own preachings, simply serving as "a sample and an example" for those who wished to lead the life he preached. The bylaws now openly listed him as "supreme spiritual authority" while requiring that he be called by the various terms used to describe God. Divine thus sought to preserve officially and for all time the aura that had marked his personal rule just as the Peace Mission entered a new, more impersonal stage of its existence.

Incorporation improved the long-range legal position of the Peace Mission, but it could not ward off the menace that the Brown case posed. Those court proceedings were like a vise that squeezed ever more tightly the Peace Mission's operations, until by mid-1942, Divine faced the apparent choice of meeting Brown's financial claim or going to prison. Typically, he discovered a third alternative no one else had foreseen.

In July 1942, Father Divine left New York permanently. Vowing never to pay an "unjust" judgment, he relocated with several hundred followers in Philadelphia, safely beyond the legal limits of New York authorities. He thus frustrated Verinda Brown's demands and the threat of imminent imprisonment. Yet the cost was high: isolation from the heart of his Harlem-based movement.

Father Divine's sudden departure from New York, coming just when a return of national prosperity and high employment were weakening the Peace

Protesting a judge's ruling in the Verinda Brown case, placard-bearing Divine supporters assemble at the New York Supreme Court Building. No mere legal judgment against the cult leader could shake the unquestioning trust of his followers, who literally regarded him as God.

Mission's economic appeal, led to a sharp decline in his following. Yet this appeared not to affect Divine greatly, for he was by then becoming absorbed with the details of his new corporation, to the increasing neglect of mass-based activity. After years of unrelenting work for reform, he seemed almost to welcome a new stage of serenity and withdrawal from an often hostile society.

Then, too, by the time he quit Harlem, Father Divine was already entering old age—not so suddenly as to threaten his hold over the Peace Mission, but leading him nevertheless to measurably slow the pace of his leadership. The years in Philadelphia therefore did not witness a revival of Divine's Peace Mission movement but rather its quiet consolidation as old legal claims faded away and new social currents passed it by.

During this period, the once vital economic life of the Peace Mission waned. Most of its businesses outside Philadelphia, Newark, and Harlem eventually closed down, including those in the vaunted Promised Land, whose properties were largely sold off. The main problem, which worsened with the years, was not that the businesses were unprofitable; rather, the continued economic benefits of cooperation no longer seemed a sufficient reason in these prosperous times to give up everything for Father Divine. In short, as few converts joined the movement and as old disciples left or shifted from rural branches back to the cities, a once bustling multimillion-dollar cooperative network dissolved for lack of people to manage it.

As the Peace Mission lost its former scope and influence, it compensated by seeking recognition as a legitimate religious institution. There arose new orders of devoted disciples, each with a distinctive code of conduct and special rituals. Rosebuds included young women disciples, Lily-buds somewhat older women, and Crusaders men of all ages. If one already lived a celibate life, as Father Divine advocated, it was not difficult to become a member in one of these orders: About half the active disciples belonged.

Nor were these privileged orders, except for the right to lead hymns of praise to Father Divine. New recruits in these orders did, however, wear special uniforms, brightly colored to distinguish them from the other members of the Peace Mission. It was a small move, perhaps, but it highlighted the change in the Peace Mission from a spontaneous evangelical gathering to a formal, established church.

Another sign of the movement's age and growing conservatism was its thorough reinterpretation of the religious meaning of death. Father Divine for many years had preached that a person of perfect faith would always enjoy perfect physical health. Death had therefore seemed to Peace Mission members the ultimate disgrace, resulting from a sinful state of mind. This teaching was so ingrained that when Father Divine's wife of many years, Pinninah, died in 1937, he avoided informing his disciples for fear that the news might shatter their faith.

Yet as the deaths of veteran followers became more frequent, Father Divine began to refer to death as a natural process indicating that a person's spirit had sought to obtain a new and more perfect body. This drastically altered view of immortality as mainly spiritual fit more closely with traditional Christian notions as well as with the movement's growing willingness to look for perfection in a coming life rather than in the present.

It is symbolic of the Peace Mission's new, inward-looking character that Father Divine's one brief return to fame came with a deeply personal act. In August 1946, he appeared in his Philadelphia church with a beautiful 21-year-old white disciple called Sweet Angel and announced that he had secretly married her more than 3 months earlier. The interracial aspect of the marriage drew headlines across the country, and astonished disciples tried to come to grips with the news that their leader, after years of solitary rule, was now preparing to share the glory, if not the power, of his kingdom.

The marriage amazed all the more because the bride, born Edna Rose Ritchings in Canada, was scarcely known to anyone in the Philadelphia church before late 1945. At that time, she made a pilgrimage by bus from a West Coast Peace Mission center to visit Father Divine. Although Sweet Angel left for Montreal when her numerous visa extensions were discontinued, she overcame both parental objections

The second Mother Divine—formerly known as both Edna Rose Ritchings of Canada and Sweet Angel—exchanges an affectionate glance with her new husband soon after their 1946 wedding. Almost a half-century older than his 21-year-old bride, Divine told disciples that she was the "reincarnation of the spirit" of the first Mother Divine, who had died 9 years earlier.

and bureaucratic barriers to return to Philadelphia. She recalled many years later, "I just wanted to come down to see Father." The day after her arrival he married her.

The marriage raised some difficult questions among the faithful, including what had happened to Mother Divine, who had simply disappeared from view in 1937. No one until now had dared question her whereabouts, but Father Divine's new marriage made at least some explanation necessary, to ensure the continued morale of followers taught to believe that the virtuous would never die.

Divine assured his followers that his was not a marriage in the conventional sense but a spiritual union to symbolize interracial harmony and uphold a standard of chaste conduct for others in the movement. As for Mother Divine's fate, he declared that she had desired a new, more beautiful Rosebud body and had been reincarnated as Sweet Angel, his new wife. This was a challenging concept for anyone who remembered the dark, heavyset form of the elderly Mother Divine and then looked at the blond, youthful Sweet Angel. The disciples accepted their leader's assurances, however, that "Mrs. Divine presently, as you see her," is the "reincarnation of the spirit" of Mother Divine.

In addition to providing Father Divine a personable, enthusiastic, utterly devoted companion, the marriage also aided the Peace Mission's transition from cult to church: It provided for a successor to Father Divine. This was an accomplishment carefully left unspoken, for disciples took their leader's continued existence as a certainty, nor could they

In 1968, 3 years after Divine's death at age 86, followers interred his body in this marble mausoleum. Described by one contemporary architect as "probably one of the finest structures of its kind anywhere in America," the tomb cost $250,000, paid by Divine's faithful flock.

then imagine the Peace Mission except in terms of Father Divine's presence. Still, by designating Sweet Angel as his "spotless virgin bride" who represented his "church" on earth, Divine gave her the authority needed to eventually rule in his stead.

By 1960, the daily administration of the Peace Mission had fallen to the second Mother Divine, working closely with Father Divine's able secretarial staff. Although not an innovator or social crusader, as Father Divine had been in his prime, she had already shown herself well suited to lead the Peace Mission in its search for spiritual purity and organizational stability. Mother Divine made an impressive, intelligent, dignified presence at Peace Mission banquets and a gracious diplomat to guests from all walks of life. It was clear that Father Divine's earlier social radicalism was to be merely revered, not revived. But within the Peace Mission's own centers, the Father's vision of a chaste, integrated communal society would go on as before.

Father Divine survived into the 1960s only as a feeble remnant of his once vigorous self. His last public appearance was in 1963, and on that occasion the 84-year-old Father merely watched as Mother Divine gave the banquet sermon and welcomed visitors. In September 1964, after his absence from a major event, his secretaries publicly hinted that his death was not far off. Three of his closest aides reported that they saw Father Divine daily but that they were prepared for the day when he would not be continually with them.

The civil rights movement entered its most dynamic stage during these years, but the Peace Mission's involvement in the cause had by then faded to a wholly passive state. In the absence of reform activities by the ailing Peace Mission leader, his disciples simply celebrated the harmony they had always known in their Father's kingdom. As one follower, Blessed Mary Love, explained in 1964, "Father has freed us from within."

There were signs that the aged Father Divine himself was not nearly so content to ignore the nation's great social upheaval. Possibly frustrated by his inability to play a personal role in the civil rights struggles, he compensated by taking credit for developments he approved of without having participated in them directly. In that vein, he suggested that his spirit had inspired the actions of the interracial Freedom Riders and sit-in demonstrators as well as other campaigns challenging segregation in the South. Divine wrote to a disciple in July 1961, "You can see the work of my spirit moving among men in all parts of the world. . . . I am stirring up the racial issue in Africa; and in the deep South of this country I am bringing about a true democratic feeling of mutual understanding concerning the same rights of each and every inhabitant of this nation."

The continued force of Father Divine's interest in civil rights became fully evident after President Lyndon B. Johnson delivered a ringing speech in March 1965 urging passage of the voting rights bill. This measure would provide the federal government with much stronger powers to enforce the voting rights of any citizen, regardless of race, creed, or color; it was a step Divine had urged for three decades. Despite his extreme frailty, Divine rallied his reserves of physical strength to convey his heartfelt support for the president's commitment. He wrote to Johnson:

> I highly commend you on your wonderful speech before the Joint Session of Congress. It is with profound gratitude I have witnessed this great ship of state being steered into a new world of unity and dignity for all mankind. If this "so great a people" will now stand together just as Americans in the unity of spirit, mind, of aim and of purpose, there is

nothing that can prevent the establishment of a universal Utopian democracy in which all men, everywhere, shall enjoy the reality of life, liberty, and happiness. May I extend my blessings as my life to you in this effort.

Within six months, Father Divine died. He was then 86 and convinced that the interracial utopia for which he had so long yearned was at last coming to pass. Whatever the accuracy of that judgment, the evidence does suggest that in the cause of racial harmony and equality he had indeed, with considerable effect, extended his blessings and his life. ❧

Divine's widow (center, facing camera) waits out disciples' applause before beginning a sermon. The second Mother Divine, who had started managing the Peace Mission in the early 1960s, was still at the helm in the 1990s.

CHRONOLOGY

———— ❦ ————

1879	Father Divine is born George Baker in Rockville, Maryland
1906	Joins forces with the preachers John Hickerson and Samuel Morris
1912	Begins to preach on his own under the name the Messenger
1914	Arrested in Valdosta, Georgia, for blasphemy
ca. 1915	Arrives in the Harlem district of New York City
ca. 1919	Settles in Sayville, New York; marries Pinninah, one of his disciples; begins to call himself Major J. Divine
ca. 1930	Launches the Peace Mission movement; provides Sunday banquets for the poor
1931	Arrested in Sayville for disturbing the peace
1932	Convicted and sentenced to a year in prison; released on bail; relocates to Harlem
1933	New York State Supreme Court unanimously overturns the guilty verdict
1935	Father Divine launches the Promised Land rural cooperative project in New York's Ulster County
1936	Issues the Righteous Government Platform
1937	Pinninah dies
1938	Peace Mission members acquire land bordering President Franklin Roosevelt's estate in Hyde Park, New York
1940	Father Divine's followers gather a quarter of a million signatures on a petition urging passage of an antilynching law
1942	Peace Mission members purchase beachfront property in Brigantine, New Jersey; Father Divine relocates to Philadelphia
1946	Marries Edna Rose Ritchings, who is also called Sweet Angel and Mother Divine
1961	Blesses the Freedom Rides and other civil rights campaigns
1965	Dies in Philadelphia and is succeeded by Mother Divine as head of the Peace Mission movement

FURTHER READING

Braden, Charles Samuel. *These Also Believe: A Study of Modern American Cults and Minority Religious Movements.* New York: Macmillan, 1949.

Burnham, Kenneth E. *God Comes to America: Father Divine and the Peace Mission Movement.* Boston: Lambeth Press, 1979.

Fauset, Arthur Huff. *Black Gods of the Metropolis: Negro Religious Cults of the Urban North.* 1944. Reprint. Philadelphia: University of Pennsylvania Press, 1971.

Harris, Sarah. *Father Divine.* 2d ed. New York: Collier Books, 1971.

Hoshor, John. *God in a Rolls Royce: The Rise of Father Divine, Madman, Menace, or Messiah. . . .* New York: Hillman-Curl, 1936.

McKelway, St. Clair, and A. J. Liebling. "Who Is This King of Glory?" *New Yorker* (June 13, 1936): 21–28; (June 20, 1936): 22–28; (June 27, 1936): 22–32.

Parker, Robert A. *Incredible Messiah: The Deification of Father Divine.* Boston: Little, Brown, 1937.

Washington, Joseph R., Jr. *Black Sects and Cults: The Power Axis in an Ethnic Ethic.* New York: Doubleday, 1973.

Watts, Jill Marie. "'Shout the Victory': The History of Father Divine and the Peace Mission Movement, 1879–1942," Ph.D. diss., University of California, Los Angeles, 1989.

Weisbrot, Robert. *Father Divine and the Struggle for Racial Equality.* 1983. Reprint. Boston: Beacon Press, 1984.

Young, Henry J. *Major Black Religious Leaders Since 1940.* Nashville: Abingdon, 1979.

INDEX

PICTURE CREDITS

———— ❧ ————

ROBERT WEISBROT, a native of New York City, teaches American history at Colby College in Waterville, Maine. He is the author of *Father Divine and the Struggle for Racial Equality* (Beacon Press, 1984), cited by the journal *Choice* for outstanding achievement in biography. His most recent book is the highly acclaimed *Freedom Bound: A History of America's Civil Rights Movement* (Penguin, 1991).

NATHAN IRVIN HUGGINS, one of America's leading scholars in the field of black studies, helped select the titles for the BLACK AMERICANS OF ACHIEVEMENT series, for which he also served as senior consulting editor. He was the W.E.B. Du Bois Professor of History and of Afro-American Studies at Harvard University and the director of the W.E.B. Du Bois Institute for Afro-American Research at Harvard. He received his doctorate from Harvard in 1962 and returned there as a professor in 1980 after teaching at Columbia University, the University of Massachusetts, Lake Forest College, and the California State University, Long Beach. He was the author of four books and dozens of articles, including *Black Odyssey: The Afro-American Ordeal in Slavery*, *The Harlem Renaissance*, and *Slave and Citizen: The Life of Frederick Douglass*, and was associated with the Children's Television Workshop, National Public Radio, the Boston Athenaeum, the Museum of Afro-American History, the Howard Thurman Educational Trust, and Upward Bound. Professor Huggins died in 1989, at the age of 62, in Cambridge, Massachusetts.